Retail
Entertainment

retail
Entertainment

Martin M. Pegler

Retail Reporting Corporation
302 Fifth Avenue
New York, NY 10001

Distributors to the trade in the United States and Canada
Watson-Guptill Publishers
1515 Broadway
New York, NY 10036

Distributors outside the United States and Canada
Hearst Books International
1350 Avenue of the Americas
New York, NY 10019

Library of Congress Cataloging in Publication Data:
Retail Entertainment

Printed in Hong Kong
ISBN 0-934590-89-3

Designed by Dutton & Sherman

Contents

Sporting Goods/Sportswear

NikeTown 10

Champion 14

Runner's Choice 16

REI 18

Dick's Clothing & Sporting Goods 24

Sportmart 28

World of Sports 32

Outdoor World 36

Michael Jordan Golf 38

Arnold Palmer Golf 42

Golf Central 44

Muskoka Lakes Retail Store 46

Music/Videos

Camelot Music 50

HMV Records, New York 54

HMV Records, Oberhausen, Germany 58

Sam Goody 62

Spec's 66

Wow! 68

Blockbuster 70

Rogers' Video 74

Movie Seller 76

Computer/Electronics

Gateway 2000 80

Communication Expo 84

Comcast 88

Screenz Digital University 90

Digital 92

Microsoft USA 94

Mondo 96

Ultimate Electronics 98

Souvenirs

Warner Bros. 102

Universal Studio Store 108

Jurassic Park Retail Store 110

Viacom Entertainment Store 112

Overboard 116

Science Fiction Zone 120

Awesome Atom's Science Store 122

Hard Rock Hotel Retail Store 124

Planet Hollywood Superstore 128

Motown Retail 130

Planet Hollywood 132

CBS Store 133

Official All Star Cafe 134

Rainforest Cafe 135

Cleveland Indians Team Store 136

Ozone 140

Atlanta Braves Clubhouse Store 141

NASCAR Thunder 142

Daytona PitShop 146

Indianapolis Motor Speedway Store 150

Potpourri

Tempus 154

Transporter 158

Toys 'R' Us 160

Zoom 162

Game Keepers 164

Travelfest 166

Thomas Cook 168

F.A.O. Schweetz 170

Fuzziwigs 172

Great Cars/Great Trucks 174

Introduction

Each year seems to bring a new buzz-word to Retailing: a new concept that appears to be the basis for success. The current buzzword has been around for several years and rather than diminishing in its power, it is becoming more and more important. The "open sesame" to retail success—whether it is for the small retailer, the designer with a designer boutique, a chain store operation, department store, or mall or shopping center—is ENTERTAINMENT.

One can't open any trade magazine today without being bombarded with articles on entertainment! Entertainment is the magic word that turns time-hoarders into shoppers and shoppers into buyers. It is the excuse that can lift the couch-bound individual off the couch—away from the TV set or the web-site—into the car and off to the mall to get immersed in the excitement, the fun, the spectacle and sizzle of Entertainment.

For some time now, restaurants such as Planet Hollywood and Hard Rock Cafe have capitalized and profited from the Entertainment factor. Entertainment has now become the destination for people otherwise too busy to partake in a shopping expedition. Entertainment has become the main focus of giant malls such as Mall of America and the West Edmonton Mall in Edmonton, Canada. Many smaller malls and strip centers are being built around Entertainment venues such as super-colossal, multi-screen movie theaters or entertainment-type stores like a Disney giant, a Warner Bros. Megastore, a giant HMV or Music/Record/CD/Computer store or a sporting goods store complete with basketball court, putting green and racing oval.

What elements provide this entertainment and how these factors are incorporated into the store's design is the thrust of this book. These factors can include the color and lighting effects, the visual impact, the overscaled and sometimes overwhelming size of props and decor, the interactive displays and fixtures that beg to be touched, the music and the memorabilia collected, and even the add-on cafe or bar that provides a few moments of rest and refuge from the assault on the senses taking place within the store. Imagine trying on shoes and then testing them on a racing oval or climbing a "stone cliff" recreated in the store. How about swinging golf clubs while standing on a "green" in a miniature golf course? Today you can visit a store such as Nike that is part theater, part museum and part retail.

In this edition we have collected some of these retail solutions and also shown where shoppers are shopping and what they are shopping for. Perhaps at no other time in Retailing have "souvenirs" meant as much as they do today. Souvenirs are memories that one can hold and tangibly recall at any time: the memories can be of a restaurant, an adventure, a visit, a tour, or a moment in time.

We hope you will find this book entertaining and full of memorable moments in retailing in the '90s.

Martin M. Pegler

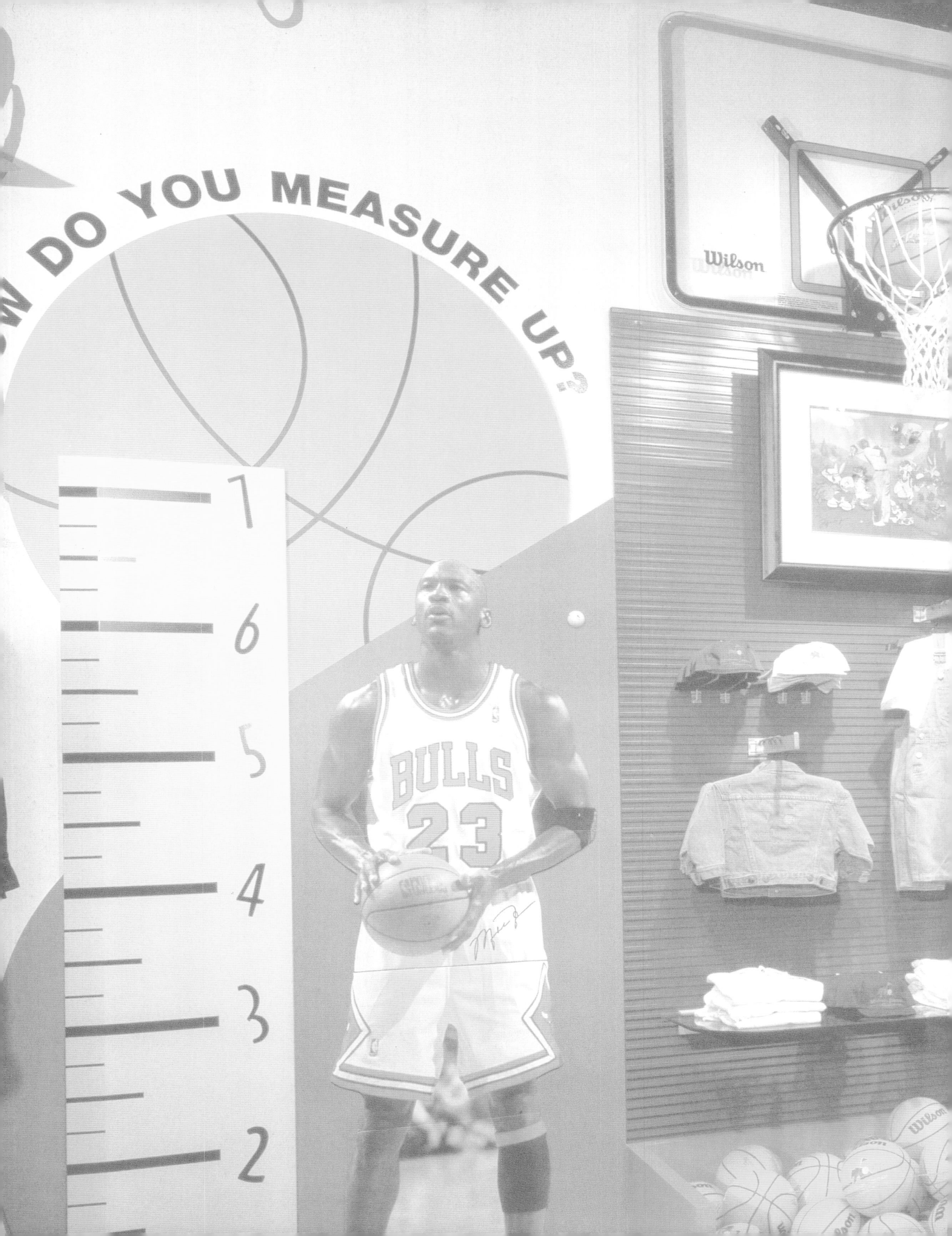
W DO YOU MEASURE UP?
Wilson
7
6
5
4
3
2
BULLS
23

Sporting Goods/Sportswear

"If it turns out my best wasn't good enough, then at least I'll never look back and say I was too afraid to try."

BE LIKE MIKE...
Play Golf!!

When Niketown opened on East 57th Street — just off Fifth Avenue — and joined the Warner Bros. store just across the street, Entertainment in Retail was firmly ensconced on 57th Street — a street already brimming over with fun theme restaurants.

"This is a store for New Yorkers and for athletes around the world: a tribute to the timeless spirit of sports." The building was conceived as a building within a building. The exterior is reminiscent of classic school gymnasiums and other historic sports facilities in New York, and the interior is a completely free-standing modern structure containing five retail floors for a total of 66,520 square feet of selling space.

The buildings come together in a central, open atrium "where the store goes through an architectural metamorphosis. "Through interactive architecture, every 20 minutes the interior atrium "morphs" from a retail space to an "inspirational/educational storytelling space." A giant screen descends over the front arched window and the atrium skylight to dim the space and one of five, three-minute Nike films is shown on the 36 feet x 22 feet media screen. Inspired by sports

Niketown

E. 57th Street, New York, NY

Design: **Gordon Thompson, V.P. of Design, Nike**

John Hoke, Image Design Creative Director

scoreboards, a Nike clock then counts down to the next film showing.

The Niketown store combines retail with entertainment and the proof is in the thousands of city citizens and the tourists who cram their way through the store. The physical space is enhanced with sports archives and memorabilia and a host of interactive media displays. A giant flipper board gives continual, up-to-the-minute sport scores from around the world while video monitors show live satellite broadcasts of sporting events.

The Swoosh information desk provides current data on nearby sporting events, clinic clubs and store events. Twenty-six shoe tubes visibly transport Nike shoes from the basement stockroom to the retail floors adding a kinetic "space" feeling to the store.

Other sources of "entertainment" for the Nike shopper are the Global Soccer Interactive display and the interactive "Air Jordan Radio" that highlights the athlete's great career through sound bites. The Athlete's Wall, located in the rear of the store and extending up from the first to the fifth floor, is filled with photos of the Nike Great. On the second, third and fourth floors the visitor can get more information about these athletes in the Athlete Bio Tower CD-ROM displays.

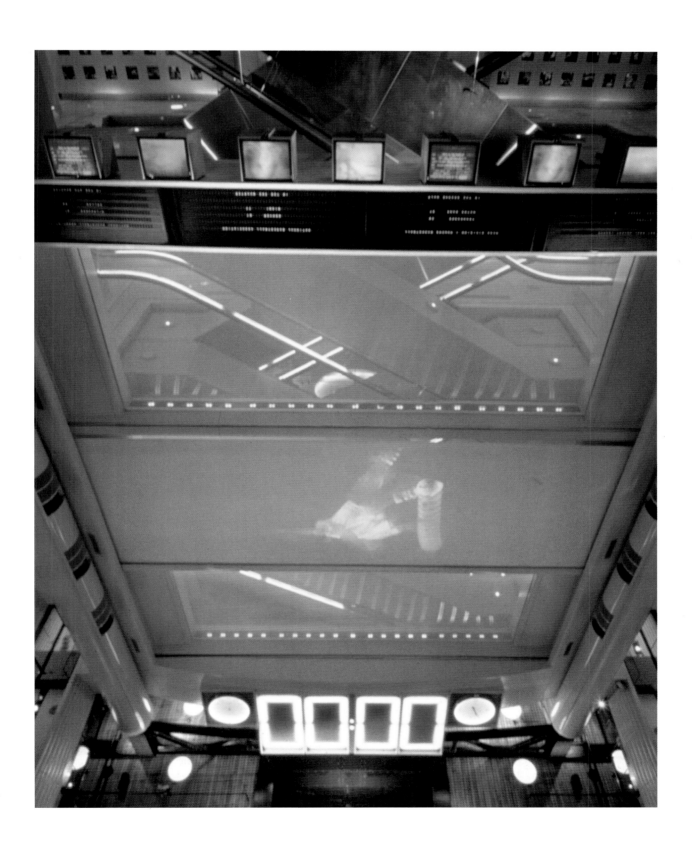

Champion

Garden State Plaza, Paramus, NJ

Design: **Bergmeyer Associates, Boston, MA**

Principal in Charge: **Joseph P. Nevin, Jr.**

Project Designer: **Ross Cromarty**

Project Manager: **Daniel Broggi**

Project Team: **Brian Anderson/Rusty Hernandez**

Environmental Graphics: **Pentagram, New York, NY**

Design: **Jane Mella**

Champion, for almost 80 years a noted name in sportswear apparel, opened its first retail store recently in the Garden State Plaza in New Jersey. The 2,300 sq. ft. space on the second level was designed by Bergmeyer Associates of Boston to house the company's men's, women's (Jogbra), children's and toddler's athletic wear. 25% of the merchandize is exclusive to the store which also carries a collection of outerwear and in-line skating apparel from the European line.

"We took a very industrial look for the fixturing of the store. The look comes from exercise machines—brushed steel finish—pulleys. It's a very dominant appearance," said Allen McNeary, Champion's Sr. V.P. of Merchandising. The storefront bows in towards the entrance and under the elliptical brushed steel canopy that carries the Champion name is the red, white and blue company logo. The natural wood floors in the store are teamed up with high-tech ceiling grills and wall fixtures that step forward into the space and resemble gym equipment with "dumb-bells" acting as merchandise displayers on the end caps. The walls are covered in a gray/white patterned material reproducing the Champion logo.

At the rear of the store is an 8 x 8 ft., three-screen billboard with 24 turning prisms. These recreate, in oversized form, images from Champion's national advertising campaigns. Also very visible and adding to the dynamics of the space are eight video monitors which show "live" professional and amateur sporting events. Some of these monitors sweep into the cash/wrap area which is enhanced with a back wall filled with basketballs restrained by net. The desk itself is finished in brushed stainless steel and red stained wood.

The dropped ceiling over the center of the store has cut outs that, like the open spaces to either side of the drop, carry some fluorescent fixtures but many more focusable spots that light up the store. Based on the success of this store and the prototype design—more Champions are on the way.

Runner's Choice

**Commerce Court, Toronto, ON
Canada**

Design: **International Design Group, Toronto, ON**

Designer: **Ronald J. Harris**

Murals: **Anselmo Art Studios, Toronto, ON**

To create a new look for Runner's Choice at a new location—the business district of Toronto—the design firm, International Design Group, accepted the challenge to conceive a store that would be a departure from mainstream sports goods retailing. The basic premise was "to bring the urban outside into the retail interior." This was achieved by creating a series of interlocking departments and boutiques where a variety of sporting goods merchandise could be effectively presented. Both circular patterns of black granite define specific areas and also affect a sense of motion while the black vertical poles establish a design rhythm. A special concrete floor was poured to simulate the streets for outdoor running shoes and a vinyl "wood" floor serves as the testing grounds for indoor shoes.

To attract women shoppers, a boutique is located just inside the entranceway. Centrally located is the cash/wrap—a visual feature of the store. It is surrounded by a "raceway" that eases the traffic flow, and directly behind it—on a raised platform—is an information/meeting area open to runners and runner groups. This is the "heart" of the store's design and located to either side are the shop's anchor departments with service areas.

The color and material palette is mostly neutral and "representative of the running environment." This color/material scheme was selected to complement the colorful merchandise. Blues and greens are used throughout as accent colors to recall the out-of-doors ambience. Maple wood is used to soften the look of the high-tech stainless steel that is used to display the running shoes. Small amounts of metallic silver slate also add sparkle and texture to the vinyl/wood and the poured concrete floors. The display panel system is suitable for face-out displays and all of the floor fixtures are on wheels and portable—"to strengthen the idea of movement."

A hand painted convex planet and blue neon illuminate the high ceiling. The circular yet varied ceiling discs also add dimension to the space while the light valences and walls add a human scale to the merchandise. Incandescent lighting, within the wall valence, maintains the true color of the merchandise and the recessed blue neon uplighting illuminates the heavens and serves as a "grow" light for the Benjaminia trees used to energize the space.

Adding to the running environment are the large TV monitor for sporting events, the bottled water dispensing machine, the colorful graphics and the stylized mannequins that also contrast with the architectural-like elements of the design.

REI

Seattle, WA

Design: **Mithun Partners, Seattle, WA**

This award-winning project, designed by Mithun Partners of Seattle, is the new, almost 90,000 sq. ft. flagship of the noted REI (Recreational Equipment Inc.) company. The store features the fully expanded line of gear and clothing for five major sports categories: camping, cycling, climbing, skiing and paddling.

The actual selling space of 80,000 sq. ft. is divided on two levels. The five outdoor specialty shops are located on the entrance level and the related outdoor clothing, footwear, accessories and services are on the second level. "The retail space design and materials reflects a casual natural atmosphere consistent with REI's outdoor heritage and environmental commitment." Natural light is emphasized throughout combined with energy efficient light, heating and cooling systems. The materials used are "honest" and natural: wood, stone, slate and metal.

The store is filled with interactive features that "provide customers opportunities to get the feel of muscle powered outdoor activities and the equipment right in the store." Probably most noteworthy of these "try it—you'll like it" experiences is the 65 ft. tall climbing pinnacle—the tallest standing climbing structure in the world. It stands in a steel and glass enclosed atrium and it is completely illuminated at night. Programmed theatrical lighting simulates the path of the sun. The pinnacle is the first thin shell climbing structure in North America and it contains four miles of hand shaped steel reinforcing rod and it's covered with over 1,000 modular climbing holds.

The unit incorporates a variety of climbing features like cracks, overhangs, faces, knife-edges, and it is adaptable for climbers of all abilities. The pinnacle can accommodate up to 15 climbers at a time and from the top there is a spectacular view of the Puget Sound and the Olympic

Mountains. This has become the signature element in the store design.

Not to be underplayed, the other sports also have special interactive features such as the 470 ft. outdoor bike testing track in the landscaped courtyard and the indoor footwear test trail—25 ft. long by 15 ft. wide—where customers can test footwear on a variety of simulated natural terrains. For campers there are extensive displays on camping and expedition equipment, pack fitting stations, back-packing stove demonstrations, and much more.

Among the other features that make REI such a great destination for outdoors enthusiasts are: a 100 seat deli/cafe, a 250 seat meeting room for outdoor-oriented programs and special events, full service repair shops for bicycles, ski/snow boarding and paddling equipment, and a Rain Room where customers can actually test the rain gear in a make-believe rain shower.

A parent-supervised children's play area creates a sense of wilderness discovery and adventure for young outdoors persons right inside the store. An Outdoor Resource Center makes information available.

Two of the really big "natural" treats at REI are the fabulous giant rock fireplace that connects the two levels of the space and the special landscaped area around REI which features a still pond and a waterfall (charged with recirculating rainwater) amid 21,000 sq. ft. of native Northwest trees, plants and shrubs.

REI has already become one of Seattle's major tourist attractions.

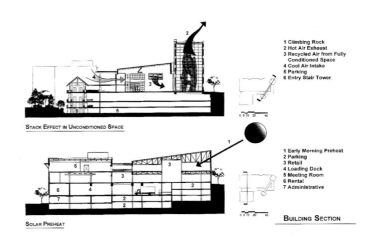

1 Climbing Rock
2 Hot Air Exhaust
3 Recycled Air from Fully
  Conditioned Space
4 Cool Air Intake
5 Parking
6 Entry Stair Tower

STACK EFFECT IN UNCONDITIONED SPACE

1 Early Morning Preheat
2 Parking
3 Retail
4 Loading Dock
5 Meeting Room
6 Rental
7 Administrative

SOLAR PREHEAT

BUILDING SECTION

The objective for the Horst Design Group was to create a sporting goods store in a two level, 800,000 sq. ft. space that would be segmented into easy-to-shop, authentic themed shops. The design would have to work well as an image for the value driven retailer whose stores are usually situated in shopping strips. In addition to creating a dramatic and memorable atmosphere, there had to be greater merchandise capabilities.

Since the store's image rests on Dick's as a prime supplier of sporting equipment, it was decided to place the assorted sporting goods departments on the upper level even though some impulse traffic would be sacrificed. The only apparel on this level is the licensed merchandise directly related to the particular branded sports gear. Men's, women's, children's and toddler's, and shoes are located on the lower level.

To move traffic down to the important ground level where the apparel and impulse material is located, a main aisle that connects the mall entrance and the down escalator is given prominence. Set to either side of this derive aisle are the special sporting goods shop of approximately 2000-3000 sq. ft. each. Each is given its own theme and look, and great care was taken as to which department was adjacent to which shop. Focal elements were also established to further the movement towards the escalator.

Dick's Clothing & Sporting Goods

Buckland Hills Mall, Hartford, CT

Design: **Horst Design Group, Huntington, NY**

Principal in Charge: **Douglas B. Horst**

Principal: **Bernhart H. Rumphorst**

Planning & Design:

Director: **Fidel Miro**

Dir. of Materials & Colors: **Cynthia Davidson**

Project Architect: **Alexander Latham**

Production Assistants: **Pat Rock/Peter Gerace/Merri Reilly**

For Dick's Clothing:

President/CEO: **Ed Stack**

Chief Operations Officer: **Bill Colombo**

V.P. of Construction: **Gary Solomon**

Photography: **Gil Amiaga, Southold, NY**

Easily seen upon entering on the second level is the 3 x 3 video wall which is suspended from the ceiling. Four towers, encircled by shelves designed for licensed caps, are situated behind the video wall. These fixtures can be adapted to support other "impulse" items depending upon the time of year. Hidden inside of each tower is an on-the-floor dressing; a smart and effective touch.

The escalator well is not only prominent in the design, it is a major focal point. Two encased conveyor belts move vertically between the floors and these shiny towers are decorated with plaques bearing the logos and brand names of the vendors whose merchandise is sold in Dick's. Also attached to these giant vertical silos are a battery of TV monitors. An illuminated simulated Olympic Torch rests on the steel truss that spans across the conveyor towers. The truss also carries an assortment of theatrical lighting equipment and also serves as the springboard for the diving figures who float over the escalator well.

Using Strizzo, an economical, pebbled conglomerate flooring material that is available in a variety of colors and has the acoustic properties of carpeting, the designers simulated an "asphalt look-alike floor near the second floor entrance and an outdoors basketball court. White Strizzo became the "ice" in the ice hockey department.

Throughout the store the theme of each department is developed on the walls and above the merchandise. A green running track with white lines surrounds the athletic shoes department and shoppers can test run on rubberized flooring material. In another area, over a painted basketball key, is a hoop where shoppers can try out their jump shots.

Dick's is pulling them in. It is a fun and exciting environment filled with interactive displays and presentations. The design is already in reproduction in nearly 1.5 million sq. ft. in various Dick's locations.

Sportmart

Lombard, IL

Design: **Schafer Associates, Oakbrook Terrace, IL**

Chairman/CEO: **Robert W. Schafer**

Project Director: **Beth Howley**

Project Planner: **R.H. Lubben**

Project Designer: **Jeff Stompor**

Sr. Graphics Designer: **Lisa Ballwasser**

Graphics Designer: **Andrea Schindleback**

Project Manager: **Walter Plavsic**

The 45,000 sq. ft. Sportmart "takes the sports category and turns it into a celebration of youth reflecting the lifestyle of today's young savvy participants and those who aspire to do it." The prototype store combines hardgoods and softgoods together into four "worlds" of sport.

Visible from the entrance—down the single main concourse of the store—are the different "worlds": each is characterized by "in-your-face" billboards and vertical pylons carrying the "world's" identification. The concourse is highlighted with sporting activities and the materials used include industrial diamond plate stainless steel floors and an expanded metal accessories ceiling treatment set askew to the walls, the aisles and the world identifiers.

Each "shop" has its own unique attitude and is still "hip, high-energy and urban." The Nike shop with apparel and top-of-the-line footwear is an anchor and focal point at the end of the concourse. At the far end, a 20 ft. internally-illuminated rotating signboard carries Sportmart's tag line, "60,000 Kinds of Adrenalin" along with Nike's swoosh and "Just do it" logo.

Up front, near the entrance is "Suit Up" which suggests the excitement of team sports. The basketball shop, here, has scoreboard monitors, a court area and replicas of basketball players' shoe sizes and hand prints. Wood basketball flooring is combined with 3M's one-side viewing material on which oversized graphics are printed, expanded metal, mdf (particle board), and the "Suit Up" signature blue color which appears on its pylon and the end caps of the fixtures appearing in this area.

Located within "Golf Club" is a swing room called "Tee Off" which is complete with a wrap around 3M "virtual reality hole." There is a putting green to test the product and the shopfronts within the space give the "Club" its own ambience in which to show off Sportmart's private label of golfing apparel. This area is finished in cherry stained mdf with black accents and sisal carpeting.

The cool attitude of a workout club sets the theme for "Burn It." A four-foot floor grid of rubber matting set on a dynamic angle to the concourse, stainless steel panels behind the merchandise and diamond plate lighted treadmill platforms are used along with the multi-purpose fixtures to dress the area for "a compelling fitness story."

The out-of-doors lifestyle sets the theme for "Get Out." The center pod is anchored by a bold pattern of wood slats and the shaped "hat," unique to this "world's" identifier, is reminiscent of a tent's shape. As in the other areas, mdf (particle board) towers are used to highlight the footwear for the category.

"Lace Up" is the area for self-service shoes. Here, the materials include mdf, troweled concrete marlite panels on the identifier and a blue Forbo vinyl oval anchors the center pod. The massive soles of the newest Nike shoes appear on all four of the tail perimeter end caps.

Educational videos flank the perimeter walls and a vertical pylon graphic instructs customers on how to purchase a product. There is even a rubber oval track for those who would test in-line skates. The LX logo is used to indicate the Sportmart brand and it is painted on the sidewalk outside the store. It serves as "a rating vehicle for private label product in a best-in-class philosophy; and is the brand label (LX Legacy) for Sportmart's new golf apparel."

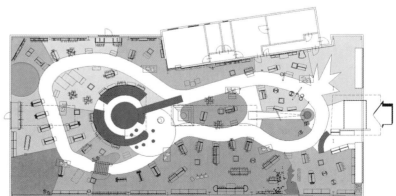

World of Sport

Fulda, Germany

Design & Store Fittings: **Umdasch Shop Concept GmbH, Bolzano, Italy**

Architect: **Bernd Keib, Fulda, Germany**

Merchandising: **Deko Design, Bad Salzschlierf**

Photography: **Umdasch Shop Concept, Amstetten, Austria**

In the area of Fulda, in Germany, a large and growing market has developed that is sports oriented. To satisfy the needs of this group, the World of Sport was created. The designers and the fixture/fitting supplier are all part of the Umdasch Shop Concept Group.

The large rectangular plan covers one main floor with an office located on a mezzanine. A giant undulating loop provides the major access around the floor and exciting and unique visual effects have been incorporated into the loop's design to entertain, instruct and interest the shopper on the way. Each sport or sporting activity has its own special setting in the high ceilinged hall and the spaces are further differentiated by the changing patterns and materials used on the floors.

The design firm, Umdasch Shop Concept GmbH, is internationally known as a manufacturer of many fine and adaptable floor and wall fixturing/fitting systems. For the World of Sport, the designers used their "neutrally designed" Quadra system for the wall areas an in the "middle shop."

In conjunction with this flexible system the designers have used an assortment of materials (tile, natural and varnished woods, metal, etc.) on the walls to specialize the looks of the individual shops within the store.

For the hung and folded garments, out on the selling floor, classic gondolas on tiered pedestals were used. In the shoe department the "Flat" perforated steel fixture system served to show off the assortment while it also added to the scene.

The lighting in the store combines the natural daylight that filters in through the skylights cut into the industrial-type ceiling with metal shaded drop lights hanging off posts along the snaking loop aisle and myriad fluorescent tubes suspended in a random, jack-straw pattern from the ceiling.

Outdoor World

Sawgrass Mall, Sunrise, FL

Architect/Design: **Blitstein Design, Coral Gables, FL**
Peter Blitstein

Interior Design: **Ellen House**

Contractor: **RCC, Deerfield Park, FL**

Photography: **Jim Stillman**

Located in the popular tourist destination, Sawgrass Mall in Sunrise, FL, is Sam Zackowitz's new Outdoor World. Zackowitz, an operator of six traditional Army/Navy stores in Florida, broke precedence and "re-engineered a rather olive drab, aging business concept into a family-oriented store apt to attract as many women as men and also appeals to the fast driven taste of teens looking for something new and different."

It starts off out front. Instead of the usual heavy and overwhelming stuffing of merchandise into the windows, there are video monitors promoting an in-store shooting range (using paint guns) and a mechanical climbing wall for hearty "suburban mountain climbers" looking for a physical challenge.

Ellen Houser working with architect/designer Peter Blitstein and the RCC contractors of Deerfield Park created a "utilitarian '90s high-tech concept with easily defined sections enhanced with interactive TV monitors that either display merchandise or illustrate use through fashion shows.

The centrally located steel mezzanine display is the focal point of the design and it showcases colorful tents and defines other areas in the store. White mannequins wearing the store's clothing seem to appear everywhere adding excitement to the shopping floor. An industrial framework and shelving system effectively complements the casual sportswear and the outdoor/camping equipment and accessories. Footwear, a big seller, utilizes an interactive kiosk video display which allows shoppers to select brand, style, color and size.

Throughout, the designers used military memorabilia-like World War II vintage address-o-graph machine which still turns out embossed "dog tags" that are a great fashion accessory for teenagers. Rifles, handguns and knives are not shown or sold here though teddy bears dressed in uniforms of the assorted branches of the armed services are popular with the shoppers.

Interestingly, 60% of the shoppers at Outdoor World are women who are attracted by the quality and the discounted prices on the top brand merchandise. It doesn't hurt that it is also a fun and funky place for the whole family to shop.

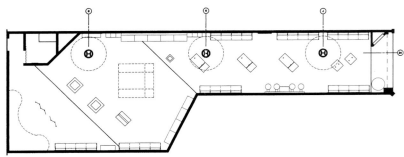

Michael Jordan Golf Co.

Woodfield Mall, Schaumburg, IL

Design: **Hanna Design Group, Rolling Meadow, IL**

President: **Michael C. Hanna**

Creative Director: **Rose Tejeda-Navarre**

Sr. Project Architect: **Mel Cea**

Graphic Designer: **Kathy Bilica**

Intern Architect: **Mike Richardson**

Michael Jordan Golf Co. Team:

President: **Chuck Reeves**

V.P.s: **Steve Skinner/Ann Burton**

Props and Decoratives: **Landmark Studio, Muskegon, MI**

Photography: **John R. Shelves, Summit Studio, Chicago, IL**

Everybody knows that the name Michael Jordan and basketball are synonymous, but Michael Jordan and golf? For people in the Chicago area it is no secret that their hometown here is also a golf enthusiast and so this new store in the upscaled mall in Schaumburg, IL is a wild, funny and funky mix of basketball and golf as immortalized by the signature giant basketball perched atop the equally overscaled golf tee. To clarify the mix of sports even more, the store also features other MJ sports memorabilia.

The store is only 14 ft. wide in the front half, so the designers, Hanna Design Group, left much of the frontage open and uncluttered. The previously-mentioned basketball on tee totem is located up front and it cleverly disguises three structural columns within the space. The storefront is framed by a column filled with golf balls and a light box for graphics.

To accommodate the narrow entrance, the designers focused on wall-hugging fixtures so as not to visually close up the front. The perimeter fixtures are a system of vertical wood posts and arched headers which allude to basketball backboards. The same header detail enhances the floor fixtures and autographed MJ items—in custom designed glass cases—serve as end-caps. The brightly-colored and inter-active wall presentation of MJ Kidz, the children's line of merchandise, is featured in the forward part of the store.

Visible from the front is the cash/wrap and monitor ring in the rear of the space. The flooring here emulates a basketball court and it serves to complement the overscaled photographic image of the Slam Dunk poster behind the third column. This end of the store is reserved for gifts and accessories, hats and T-shirts and other souvenir items. The shoe fixture is a take-off on MJ's basketball locker.

A 30 x 12 ft. photographic collage on the rear wall is a major focal point of the design. Dimensional duotone images are superimposed over a crowd background and the text boxes and lettering are also in relief. "The collage conveys worldwide admiration for Michael Jordan while also depicting MJ's love of golf." The collage serves as a backdrop to the miniature, two-hole putting green.

Arnold Palmer Golf Center

Tahguitz Creek, CA

Design: **Design Forum, Dayton, OH**

Project Designer: **Corbin Pulliam**

Project Manager: **Rob Andrews**

Graphic Designer: **Heidi Miller**

Photography: **Barbara White, Laguna Beach, CA**

Working with the Arnold Palmer Golf Management Co., the retail design firm Design Forum of Dayton, OH has created a prototype design for the Arnold Palmer Golf Center which includes a Pro Shop and Traditions— A Golfer's Cafe. "The critical objective was to create an instantly recognizable environment that immerses the golf enthusiast in the spirit of the game and the quality associated with the Arnold Palmer name."

The Pro Shop showcases the Arnold Palmer collectibles, historic photography and memorabilia along with the clothes and gear for the game. The focal point, the demo club display, is easily identified by the distinctive signage and the interchangeable display of golf merchandise.

The store carries a full line of golf clothing and golf equipment. The design is simple, clean and contemporary with natural wood fixtures and wall units accented with green— the color of grass and golf courses. There are areas of green grass matting for putting and golfers can take a stand to get the feel of the "Woods, Wedges & Putters." In keeping with the golf course ambience, the merchandise areas are identified by the green canvas awnings lettered in yellow that angle out from the soffit above the merchandise walls.

Traditions—a Golfer's Cafe features the same natural woods along with the signature green accents. The area provides additional entertainment for the customer along with a visual display of memorabilia related to Arnold Palmer's illustrious career.

These retail/pro/cafe stores are planned to appear on every Arnold Palmer Golf Course across the country.

Golf Central

Minneapolis, MN

Design: **Design Forum, Dayton, OH**

Design: **Bill Chidley/Chris Meyer**

Project Manager: **Andy Lehman**

Architect: **Don Rethman**

If it has anything to do with the golfing lifestyle—if it is clothes, shoes, clubs or any of the many accessories—the golf enthusiast living in the Minneapolis area is sure to find it in Golf Central, a category killer store. With a goal to become the largest supplier and outfitter for the golf industry, the prototype concept, developed by Design Forum, capitalizes on the country's love of the links.

Throughout the large, warehouse type space shoppers have many opportunities to interact with the merchandise. The store design includes a putting green, a driving range, a chipping range, and a computer generated indoor simulator. The predominantly blue and green color scheme (sky and grass) brings the outdoors inside.

Actual golf bags are lined up to create a unique vertically-striped frieze around the perimeter walls and they are accented by bands of deep green and mulberry on the white walls. The ceiling is filled with dropped halogen lights and tracks of incandescents that illuminate the wall displayed merchandise. TV monitors, above eye level, add to the activity going on in the space.

As a one-shop Golf stop, the shopper can "explore" the Tommy Hilfiger or Ashworth vendor shops to pick just the right outfit to go with the perfect club already selected. At Travel Central, the fully equipped shopper can now plan a perfect vacation at a golf resort.

Need something extra? Need some repair work on your clubs? Check in with the specialists at Club Tech. There is even an area devoted to Kids Club where they can be "dressed" and/or entertained.

"While the store offers tremendous entertainment, avid golfers can find merchandise quickly at Golf Central, so they can get back out on the course."

Muskoka Lakes Retail Store

Park City, UT

Design: **Fetz Designs, Salt Lake City, UT**

Photography: **Arch Cheney, Sale Lake City, UT/Richard Springate, Seattle, WA**

Muskoka Lakes Retail Store provides something "different" for outdoors people. The merchandise is targeted at persons 21-55—predominantly middle to upper family income—who are aware of fashion, function, quality and value and "want unique looks and are willing to pay for them." The Muskoka Lakes brand of rugged merchandise brings with it "the Indian and pioneer spirit that is the inspiration for this rugged line of clothing of timeless design with the essence of Native North America."

The merchandise mix includes specially hand knit sweaters with that rugged outdoor touch, insulated jackets "for the outdoors lifestyle," and "native influenced prints" in rich fall colors. All are geared to the outdoors enthusiast who wants to identify with the hardy outdoors man/adventurer though he or she may be actually the short term mountain biker, fly fisherman, golfer or skier.

To house and "romanticize" this brand, Fetz Designs of Salt Lake City created this prototype design that is suited to spaces of 1200-2500 sq. ft. The overall look is woody with light wood-pine and maple used along with some whole log construction. The fixturing is pine wood clad with copper metal

For ease of installation, all the wall units and the cash/wrap desk are all basically free standing and depend upon the pine post and lintel construction for support. The lintels also serve to carry the track lighting as well as some of the atmospheric props—like the overturned canoe.

The ambience is enhanced with props such as the antique tables and chairs that are mixed with retro outdoor sporting equipment: snowshoes, skis, sleds. In addition, there are authentic Indian artifacts and historical pieces along with sepia prints of the Muskoka territory.

The store is filled with natural light that floods in through the skylights and the lighting plan also calls for recessed fixtures and track lighting. The floors are natural pine and rock with some areas covered with sisal carpeting or native hand loomed rugs. When space permits, live aspen and birch trees, in planters, are incorporated into the floor layout.

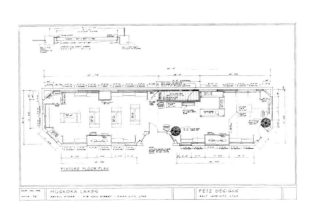

Music/Videos

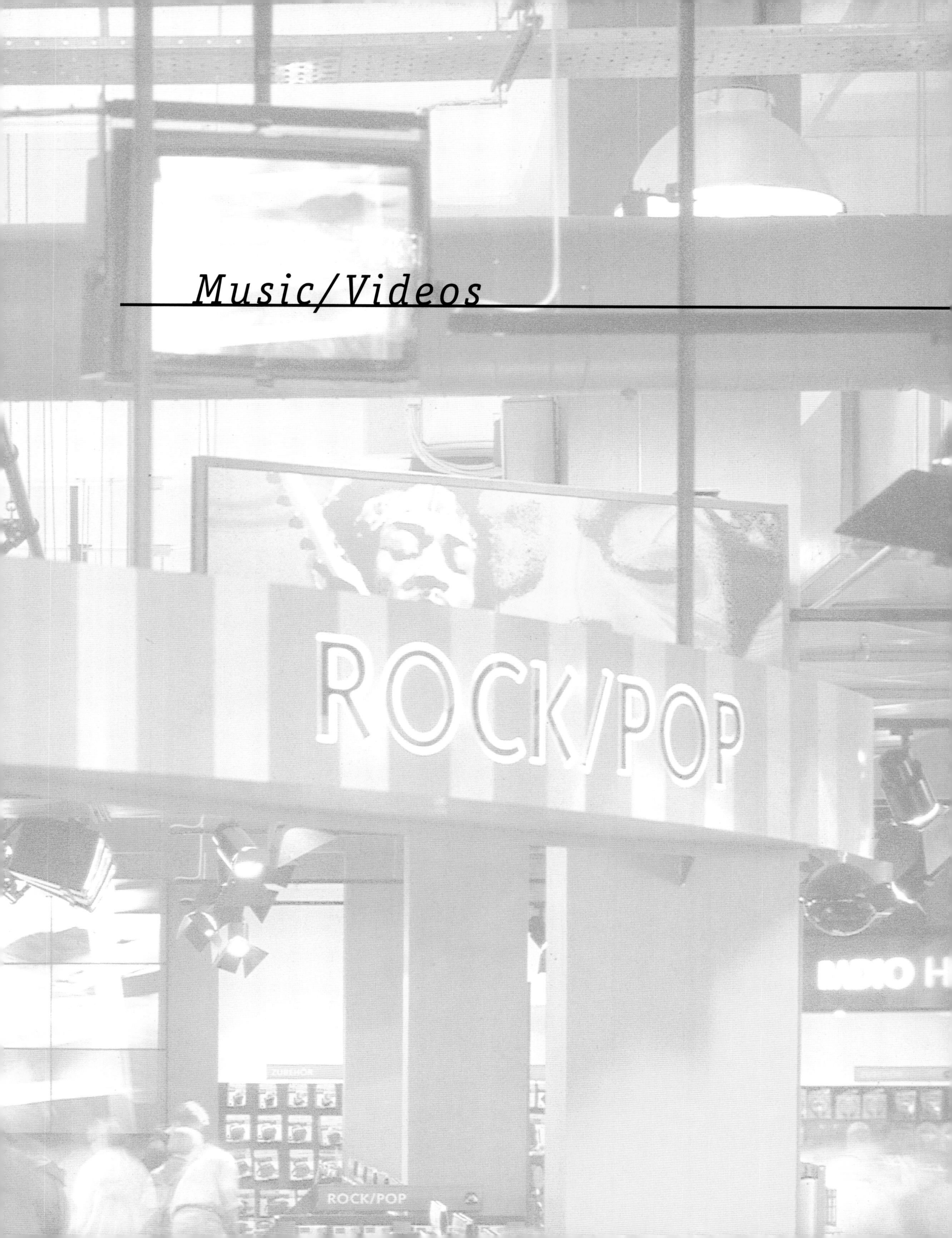

Camelot Music

Great Lakes Mall, Mentor, OH

Designer/Architect: **Jon Greenberg Associates, Southfield, MI**

C.E.O.: **Michael Crosson**

Principal-in-Charge: **Kenneth Nisch**

Planner/Designer: **Jenness Anderson**

Designer: **Michael Benincasa**

Project Manager: **Edward Kaffel**

For Camelot Music: **Kenneth Chance, V.P. Store Planning & Construction**

Photography: **In-House / Owner**

To create a new flagship and also stake out in a new competitive market, the Camelot Music Company called upon the design firm of Jon Greenberg Assoc. of Southfield, MI to originate an environment that would appeal to music lovers of all ages and genders. Rather than competing on price, Camelot wanted to stand out as an entertainment venue that provided the ultimate in service, experience and technology.

"Futuristic technology and graphics give the space its unique personality of volume and raw energy." It is the palette of intense, saturated colors that fill the large open, "industrial" space and give the store its "edge" and makes the ambience fun to shop. The lighting effects provide an authentic exhibition atmosphere with oscillating track heads and theatrical template graphics.

Bob White, senior lighting designer at Illuminating Concepts, Farmington Hills, MI—the firm that designed this store's lighting programs—said, "We used the theatrical spots to backlight fabric panels that are stretched on circular trusses that are suspended over the feature areas. The panels float in space over the product, again creating an ever-changing color palette throughout the department."

Hot Topics and top discs are highlighted with oversized number graphics with corresponding numbers inlaid in the floor in front of the Trekkian fixture displays. Instead of endless rows of CDs there are shorter, more stimulating and easier to grasp lengths of displays that allow special artists to be featured, cross merchandising opportunities and greater flexibility in getting new products out on the floor quickly.

In this light filled, musical envi-

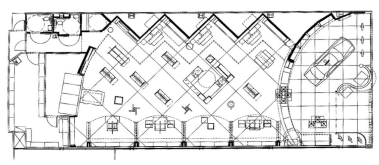

ronment that tingles with excitement, part of the entertainment is the interaction between the customer and the product. Invisible laser technology provides one of the "techno-treats." The listener is invited to step into a numbered floor circle to hear a particular "top twenty" tune. A laser beam is broken when this happens and it triggers an audio mechanism to project the music through a "sound dome" which, in turn, directs the music downwards to wash over the listener and anybody near the circle.

Contrary to the flow of Industry thinking which concentrates on teenagers and "twenty-something" as the major target market, Camelot appeals to that demographic but—with this store's design and varied sophistication—the company has a far broader attraction to age groups previously overlooked. "Experience is the magnet. Selection creates loyalty. A larger than life environment signals excitement." That's Entertainment!

HMV

Herald Square, New York
Boston, MA

Design/Architect: **Elkus Manfredi, Boston, MA**

Principal: **David P. Manfredi**

Project Manager: **Marcus Gleysteen**

Project Architect: **Alan Bruce**

Photography:

Fifth Ave.: **Mario Lorenzetti, Korab Hedrich Blessing**

Herald Square: **Chun Lai Photography**

Boston: **Warren Jagger Photography**

If one measured by sales, HMV Record Stores, a division of Thorn/EMI, is "the world's largest music retailer." To keep a competitive edge, HMV called upon the architectural design firm of Elkus/Manfredi of Boston to use store design to tell the story of HMV's values and heritage. This means showing the company's range and inventory, its "streetwise credibility" in reflecting local tastes and culture, and its values in a highly competitive merchandising area.

The designers developed a retail prototype that includes imagery and identity for specific music categories: Rock and Pop, Jazz and Classical as well as related merchandise in video and computer games. They also created a design manual; a guide line to follow in creating HMV stores around the world. The prototype design—shown on these pages in three different locations—covers about 85% of the manual with the rest left to reflect the cultural, ethnic and traditional differences of the location.

Elkus/Manfredi's design team used simple, easily available and generally inexpensive materials such as perforated metals, wood and dry wall—all in a simple, black and white neutral palette. David Manfredi said, "We use black and white with the color coming from the CDs and graphic displays." Colorful accent lighting adds to the excitement of the presentation.

The fixtures on the floor are finished mainly in black and the ceiling and ambient lighting is white. The same sense of contrast was used in showing rough against smooth textures—to separate or delineate particular spaces in the store.

Generally, materials, colors and textures vary by musical category—"reflecting the qualities of the genre." Rock and Pop are studies in contrast in materials and colors. "The materials of Jazz reflect the simple aspirational nature of its heritage and the tailored details of Classical (warm woods) strive to create an environment that is sanctuary and refuge from the world."

The Herald Square store is 21,190 sq. ft. on two levels and the Fifth Avenue store is almost as large and also features a mezzanine. The Boston store at 10,000 sq. ft. is a more traditional size. There are listening booths in all of the music areas, often at the end of the "browsers" which are designed to gently curve outward as the shelves descend so labels can be read on all shelves. Chart walls indicate what is new and video screens, moveable totems with changing graphics and music industry graphics all add excitement and color to the otherwise neutral space.

In the larger operations there are DJ booths floating in the open stairwell between the store's two levels and a performance stage for live performances. Special areas are designed for Classical, Jazz, Games and Videos.

Manfredi said, "Selling is about how much of the product is visible—how much customers can browse and how much we can make the place a destination." There is no doubt about it—HMV is a music destination.

HMV

Oberhausen, Germany

Design: **Greig + Stephenson, London, England**

Project Architect: **Ken Greig**

Project Co-ordinator: **Howard Bates**

CAD Co-ordinator: **Ewen Falconer**

Interior Design: **Ben Harker/Martyn Clarke/Robert Callis**

Graphics Designer: **Stephan Attalides**

Project Secretary: **Jo Bassi**

Joining a global chain of over 330 HMV stores around the world is this one in Oberhausen, Germany. In addition to being the first in Germany, it makes its debut in a brand new, two-level shopping center with 200,000 sq. meters of retail and leisure space. The HMV store is prominently located on the upper level of this center which anticipates a yearly traffic of over 22 million.

There is no other store quite like this HMV in Germany, and thus it immediately stands out from its competition. The designers, Greig + Stephenson of London, have employed light and graphics to create not only the ambience but to assist the shopper in making a selection. There is a readily discernable "visual vocabulary of departmental signage" that can be seen from the entrance or anywhere within the store.

The signage quickly identifies the location for any genre of music. A major portion of the store is devoted to Rock and Pop and it is this area that sets the dynamic tone for the space with its industrial blue glow of light. Other destinations are: Video Games, Singles, Jazz and other "minority" classifications of music.

Also in these areas, colored filtered light helps to define the department or sub-department. For the lovers and collectors of Classical music there is a special, acoustically isolated room with an auditorium-type ceiling that provides a respite from the high energy attitude of the rest of the store.

A state-of-the-art, flat screen video wall, at the rear of the store, seems to lessen the store's depth and makes the whole space feel more intimate and enveloping to the shopper standing out in the mall. Theatrical type lighting fixtures with adjustable barn door attachments are attached to the suspended black lighting pipes and they provide additional highlighting for the merchandise presented below, mostly on simple black racks. Also above eye level, a battery of TV monitors keep the swinging action going with non-stop entertainment.

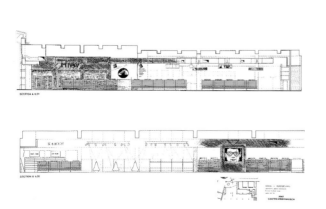

Sam Goody

Indianapolis, IN

Design: **CommArts, Boulder, CO**

Design Team: **Richard Foy/Margaret Sewell/Bryon Gough/Gillian Lewis/Davis Dute, Jr.**

Photography: **Galen Nathanson/Aaron Hoffman**

The roll-out concept for the new Sam Goody store was designed to take what was essentially a "black and neon box" that appealed to a male market aged 18-25 and re-position it as a warm, active, exciting and friendly store.

CommArts of Boulder, CO accomplished the transformation by use of a softer color palette—to attract a broader market, especially women—and with bolder and more stimulating graphics. Dominating and steering the overall design is the red, red ceiling overhead and the rich palette of autumnal colors: cranberry, red, orange, deep pinks and gold. The floor is a haphazard pattern of tiles in aqua and lavender on a creamy background. This is interrupted by a curving wood aisle that leads the shopper around the space.

Following the curved wood path overhead is a series of dropped lavender blocks. In other areas, such as in "Movies," the lavender dropped ceiling helps to distinguish the area below from the departments around it. Mauve and deep pink laminates are used to cover the curved listening desk while red and pink are combined on some of the floor racks. The cash/wrap is a mixture of the aqua and mauve laminates. Some of the walls are painted red, others are orange and gold. Under the excellent lighting the entire store glows and throbs with excitement.

"The colors, finishes, graphics and theatrical lighting created a store that is distinctive and stands out from above most other retail mall spaces." Special emphasis was placed on the perception of service and there are many listening and viewing posts positioned around the store so that shoppers can test the product before buying. The store was designed to be easy to shop and with the outstanding graphics program— it "acts as its own directory."

Spec's Music

Miami, FL

Design: **Walker Group/CNI, New York, NY**

Project Designer: **Bruce Albinson**

Graphics: **Christina Walker**

Colors & Materials: **Howard Pasternack**

To help position Spec's as the dominant music retailer in Florida, the company called upon the Walker Group/CNI to create the right retail look for this ever-increasing operation.

The Florida identity is stressed in the wave motif that is repeated throughout the exterior and interior design and graphics. "This represents the water wave image specifically linked to Florida—as well as the musical 'waves.'" The designers also selected a cool color scheme for the warm climate: soft blue-grays, sea blues and medium blues, blue-violet and accents of pastel yellow-gold. The walls, wall fixtures, slatwall panels and the floor are all in variations of the blue palette. The user-friendly, angled for better viewing, floor fixtures carry through the same colors with the addition of the soft gold color. Part of the selling floor is covered with a rippling "wave" patterned ceiling while the actual exposed ceiling is inset with fluorescent fixtures and carries track lighting along the perimeter walls.

Adding bright colors to the interior are the nine, three-dimensional murals that were created for the installation. Each one features graphics that symbolizes one of the categories of music merchandized at Spec's. These also serve as "signs" and help the customers to quickly identify the desired locations. The murals (12 x 4.5 x 1/2 ft. deep) were fabricated by J.C. Bourque and Jim Retzke of Impossible Products of Miami.

Based on the commissioned montage/illustrations by Adam Cohen who is noted for his strong colors and bold forms, the murals were executed in Gatorboard Graphic Arts board provided by International Paper.

Jeff Clifford, V.P. of Merchandising & Marketing for Spec's Music said, "We wanted to create a bright, colorful and user friendly environment for all kinds of buyers. We want the store to convey an enjoyable entertainment atmosphere—somewhat like an amusement park for your ears." That is what they got!

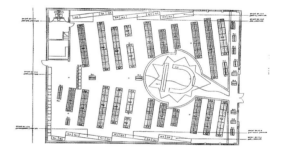

WOW! Multimedia Superstore

Long Beach, CA

Design: **Monighan & Associates, Sacramento, CA**

Principals: **Bruce Monighan/David Rickert**

Associates & Project Architects: **Paul Almond/Pam Whitehead**

In Charge of Long Beach Store: **Pam Whitehead**

Photography: **Paul Noble, Imtech, Inc.**

WOW! Multimedia Superstore is a place where shoppers can find the home entertainment of their dreams as well as the most diverse, eclectic selection of music, software, videos and books on the planet. It's about two giant retailers—The Good Guys and Tower Records—joining forces to create a truly interactive shopping experience with over 55,000 sq. ft. of space devoted to everything to do with music and entertainment.

A 200 sq. ft. video wall with "surround sound" allows shoppers to experience DSS (Digital Satellite Sound) programs, special movie screenings and live Internet events on a grandiose scale. Shoppers can also play the free slot machines—an idea that started in the Las Vegas store—at designated times with chances at winning TVs and other prizes.

Central to the whole store is the Weekly Cafe which is a cooperative enterprise with the L.A. Weekly. This award winning publication deals with news, entertainment, art and imagination. The Weekly Cafe, located in a large central atrium features net surfing and listening stations, as well as coffee, espresso drinks, smoothies, baked goods and sandwiches. The customer has two Internet and 12 music listening stations to enjoy—and hundreds of CDs to choose from. It is also the place to enjoy live music, special celebrity appearances and performances and the "World's Largest Slot Machine" which is a Pioneer Video wall system specially programmed to work as a slot machine.

Throughout the superstore there is a total of 50 listening stations, six net-surfing stations and literally thousands of CDs to sample. A dedicated music listening room provides "the ultimate listening experience" for classical, jazz and rock music aficionados. The state-of-the-art, $80,000 reference home audio studio is outfitted with components from Denon, Energy and Monster Cable—and it is for sale.

WOW! carries over 100,000 CD titles in every conceivable music genre, 25,000 videos and laser discs, over 2,000 software titles, magazines, music and pop culture books in addition to 200 brand name and 4,000 consumer electronic SKU including televisions, home and car audio, video, personal electronics, home and cellular phones and computers.

Blockbuster Video

Issaquah, WA

Design: **The Retail Group, Seattle, WA**

Principal: **J'Amy Owens**

Photography: **Craig Harrold, Seattle, WA**

The new prototype design created for Trient Partners, the owners of the Blockbuster Video franchise for Washington and Oregon, by The Retail Group starts with a surprise. The darkened entry vestibule creates a dramatic sense of anticipation while revealing a little of the "pleasures" to be found inside. The video screens, located here, show "coming attraction" trailers, complete with stereo surround sound. Inset in the floor is the Blockbuster logo while the black ceiling has been turned into a fiber optic star-lit sky.

The Director's Circle, located in the center of the store, serves as the hub for the store layout. It is staffed by a film expert who can help the shopper make a decision—or at least direct the shopper in the right direction. From here the plan follows a racetrack configuration around the perimeter of the space and it is bisected by a central drive aisle. This main aisle leads the shopper to the Preview Theater at the rear of the store where two large screens feature trailers, movie videos, and Blockbuster's corporate produced movie magazine.

The "new releases" are located on the perimeter walls and intersecting "fins," equipped with video monitors, break up the runs along the walls. The cash/wrap has been lowered to be a more comfortable and user friendly unit. It is now also a fully merchandised candy area. The gravity feed bulk candy dispensers provide the "last minute impulse purchase in a video store."

For the children there are two special areas: The TV monitor with a cartoon face and a real personality shows children's videos and in the Video Game area, the latest and "hottest" Sega and Nintendo games are showcased. Customers can play these games and even "demo" virtual reality glasses in the process.

The store's color scheme features warm, rich secondary colors such as purple and gold—to "create a compelling, dramatic interior." The designers delineated areas in the store by the flooring. Colored linoleum with graphic insets are used in the entry vestibule and at the Director's Circle while the main floor is carpeted. The perimeter "race-track" aisle is finished in genuwood.

Graphics play a vital part in the store's design and decor. Featured on a theater marquee up front in the store are floating illusionary project-ed classifications such as "mystery," "drama," "action," etc. The depart-ments are distinguished by brightly colored suspended dimensional sign-ing. The perimeter walls are enhanced with 2 x 3 ft. computer illustrations of famous movies and stars. Arranged in a montage format, they provide a backdrop for the new releases departmental signage and contribute to the exciting, theatrical atmosphere of the store."

Roger's Video

Vancouver, BC Canada

Design: **The Retail Group, Seattle, WA**

President **& Creative Director: J'Amy Owens**

Because Roger's Video has been playing #2 to Blockbuster's #1 in Canada, Roger's Cablesystem Ltd., Canada's largest cable television and movie provider, contracted The Retail Group of Seattle to "outdesign" Blockbuster Video "in order to win market share by capturing the heart, mind, soul and pocketbook of the target customer."

The overall strategy for the design firm was develop a store that "shouts Entertainment" through the use of music, scent, bolder graphics and sexier departments and merchandise zones. The goal was to make the store "fun, whimsical, exciting, dynamic and three dimensional."

Key departments are anchored by dimensional props and feature lighting. "Everything is big and bold through the use of large scale patterns and textures." The color palette for the lively store includes periwinkle, Wedgwood blue, red, sea green, marigold and black. The narrow floor-to-ceiling departmental graphics create a "shop-within-a-shop" quality in the store. Bold, overstated patterned macro graphics explode on the floor, walls, and ceiling to completely change the scale of the space.

Countdown imagery seen in movie lead-ins (5-4-3-2-1-) direct people into the store with additional iconography and movie trivia incorporated as background graphics in the store.

"New Releases" are found on the perimeter and back walls and "Feature" areas are incorporated throughout the store to prevent traffic congestion. Gondola and perimeter fixtures have been redesigned to better display product and a flexible, promotional fixture features rentals, sell-throughs and seasonal merchandise promotions. All the floor fixtures have feature end caps for highlighting award-winning and staff recommended videos.

A "game zone" floats in the sales area along with a children's "play area" and a video viewing bar. There are also video viewing stations incorporated into the New Releases walls. Within a small "shop," one can buy candy, movie merchandise, tapes and other related impulse items.

There is a "Service Counter" where questions can be answered and new customers signed up. This helps to keep the Check-Out for check out only and makes the process faster and more efficient. In order to establish a clean and easy shop environment, vendor supplied P.O.P. materials have been replaced with "Custom Zones" paid for by the vendor and each has its own unique fixturing and graphics.

Movie Seller

Toronto, Canada

Design: **Candeloro Designs Inc., Concord, Canada**

This project required "an attention-getting store front and interior" for a small mall space. The existing ceiling had to stay and the designer was also checked by the limited budget. He was able to create this fun video and movie item retail shop "that captures the excitement of cinema without having a Hollywood theme."

Using strong, vibrant colors and illuminated background fields, Pat Candeloro was able to make this store stand out from those surrounding it in the mall. He also created "a theatrical atmosphere" by integrating film symbols.

Because of the budget restrictions, inexpensive MDF, lacquer finished boards were used for all fixtures and a giant grid-type slatwall was applied to the perimeter walls.

According to the designer, "the project demonstrates that exciting dark colors can act as a complement to merchandise rather than overpower it." The space is designed with total "merchandising flexibility"; it allows many different classifications of products to be displayed around the store such as T-shirts, jackets, video tapes, laser discs, movie posters, etc.

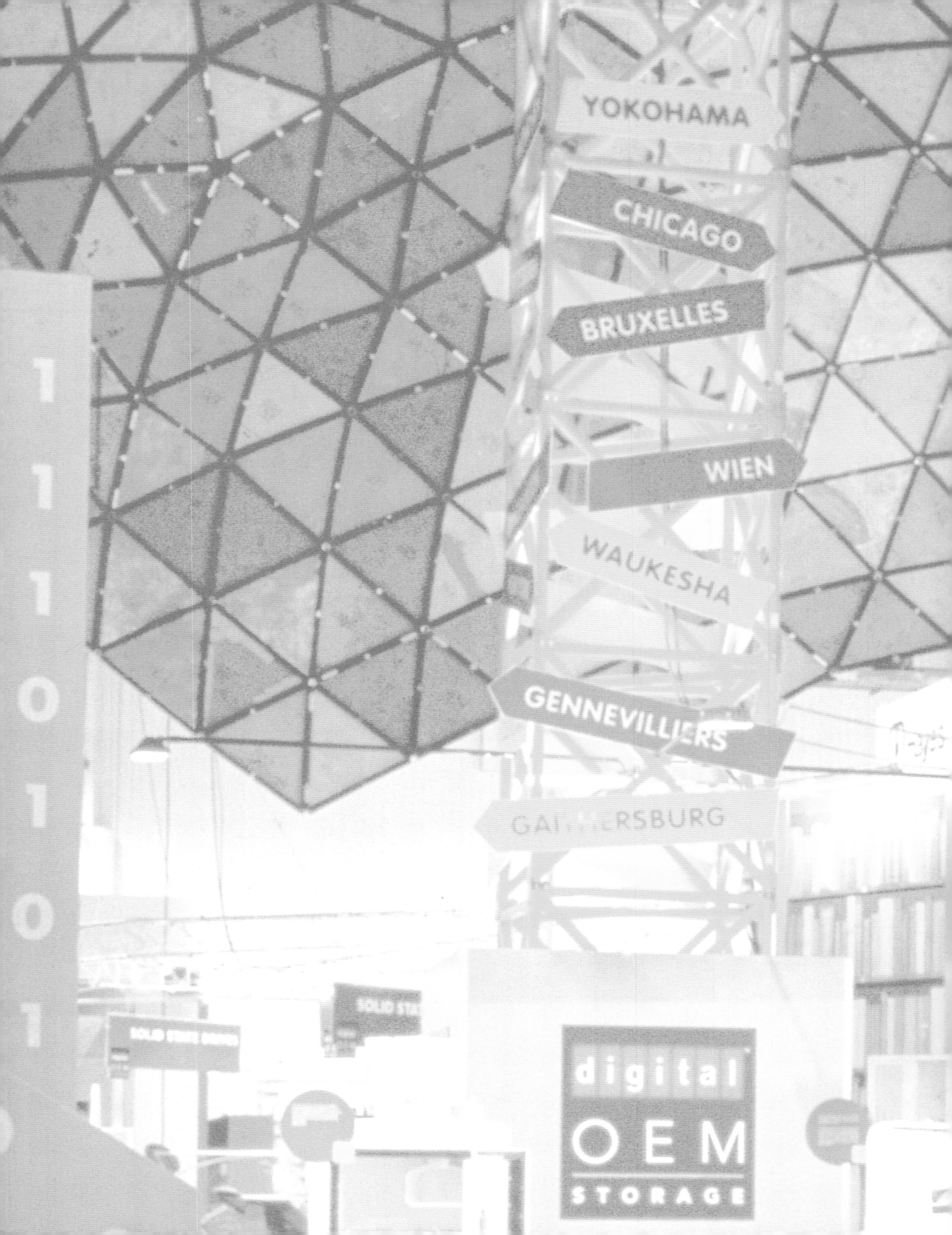
YOKOHAMA
CHICAGO
BRUXELLES
WIEN
WAUKESHA
GENNEVILLIERS
digital
OEM
STORAGE

Computer/Electronics

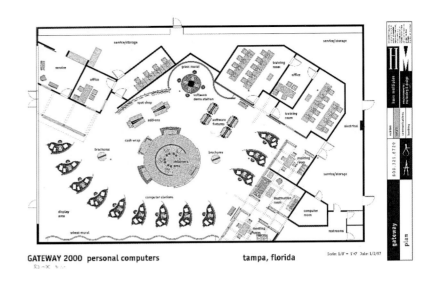

GATEWAY 2000 personal computers   tampa, florida   Scale: 1/8" = 1'-0" Date: 1/2/97

Gateway 2000 Country Store

Charlotte, NC / Orange, CT

Design: **Haas Multiples Environmental Marketing & Design, Minneapolis, MN**

President & CEO: **Tom Van Herckie**

Senior Designer: **Tim Brandow**

Photography: **Dana Wheelock, MN**

Haas Multiples of Minneapolis has taken to the country lanes and the surrounding farm lands to bring Gateway 2000's products and services into the next century. Rather than emphasizing the high technology of the products, the designers remembered that Gateway began in a barn and also by stressing the rural heartlands, they created an unusual environment that "provides a sense of comfort and security."

According to the president of Gateway 2000 of Sioux City, SD, Joseph Burke, "We wanted to create an unconventional environment for personal computer retailing while conveying the heritage of our company." Since purchasing a PC can be an anxiety-filled experience, the idea was to create a relaxed, laid-back atmosphere in which to make a decision.

The black and white splotchy design associated with Holstein cows appears on Gateway's packaging and it also dominates the interior counters and the workstations. The walls and partitions are covered with giant photomurals of rural landscapes and even the large blue display pillars are meant to suggest silos of barns that appear in the countryside. Weathered barn doors serve to close off or screen areas for conferences. Set in a barn-like structure is the Destination Room which features an entertainment type system while children have their own special space: an area inside a 12 ft. diameter silo. In the Spot Shop, merchandise is offered on pitchforks and for those who sit at one of the Holstein splattered work stations, tractor seats are provided for convenience, for fun and to further the rural imagery.

Combined in this truly unique 5000 sq. ft. setting are panels of weathered wood, corrugated metals, rusted iron, raw concrete, blue silo metal and steel. Though most of the floor is concrete, there is sisal carpeting around the cash/wrap, in the "barn" and in and around the children's silo. The concept of interactive display and selling is subtly apparent throughout. As Joseph Burke said, "The store design accurately reflects our corporate culture, the essence of what Gateway is and stands for. It's totally unlike anything the competition is doing."

Communications Expo

Parkway Shopping Center, Addison, TX

Design: **Fitch, Worthington, OH**

Project Manager: **Mark Artus**

Design Team: **Jon Baines/Fred Goode/Steve Pottschmidt/Mindi Trank/Mark Uskavitch/Catherine Bergart/Kathleen Goode/Paul Lycett/Steve Borman**

Photography: **Mark Steele, Fitch**

According to the designers of Communications Expo, Fitch of Worthington, OH, this is a new value-added retail concept developed by the same group that created COMP USA. "Communications Expo wants to solve consumer's communications problems vs. Sell technology." The objective for the designers, was to integrate telecommunication-related products with services to provide effective solutions for small businesses, home offices and individual consumers. Thus, a retail environment was designed that helps shoppers navigate their way through the space.

The hub of the 21,000 sq. ft. store is the service area—the Just Ask desk—and the floor was designed to draw people to this area. Stations are set up around this area: organized around communications solutions based on lifestyle needs. On one side, solution pods set up theoretical problems and suggest solutions. These pods are identified by signage such as "life at home," "on the move" and "business management."

In other areas, products are displayed more traditionally: by phones, monitors, keyboards, etc. All products that appear in the "solutions" are merchandised within that area and can be purchased as a "package." On the other side of the service center there are software, books and cellular phones on display.

By the use of "questions & answers" displays spaced throughout

the store, customers can find solutions for their personal technology needs. To speed up the time and ease the effort of shopping, there are 40 workstations that are fully equipped with operable products for consumers to examine and use before purchasing.

Much though went into reducing the feeling of a "warehouse" setting. Though the space is still slightly industrial, the overall feeling is comfortable. The floors are blue/green stained cement and the interior walls are painted, red, purple, lily, gray and black. Soft industrial lighting filters down from the high, wood beamed ceiling and the colorful signage stands out in eggplant, royal blue, turquoise, green, red and orange. A marbled brown linoleum covers the floor in the Help Desk and Service Desk areas. The desks are faced with a light, natural wood veneer.

Communications Expo features over 4000 products from more than 450 brands and all services and products can be demonstrated using the 400 telephones and 100 computer systems that are set up within the store.

LIFE AT HOME
SOLUTIONS

Do you have Kids?
Need to get
organized?
Are you interested
in getting more
involved with
your community?

ON THE MOVE
SOLUTIONS

PEOPLE IN BUSINESS

Just ask!

CALLER ID

28 SOFTWARE
MATH/SCIENCE
ART/CREATIVITY
ACTION/ADVENTURE
EDUCATE/ENTERTAIN

SOFTWARE
PHONE BOOKS
ATLAS
CAREER DEVELOPMENT

BOOKS & MAGAZINES

COMMUNICATION EXPO

Starter-Kit

Comcast Communications Center

King of Prussia, PA

Design: **Charles E. Broudy & Assoc. P.C., Architects, Philadelphia, PA**

Principal in Charge: **Charles E. Broudy**

Project Manager: **Michael Broudy**

V.M. Director: **David Lewis Schwing**

Project Team: **Edward Einhouse/David Schwing/ Carl Guittilla/David Ade**

Photography: **Matt Wargo, Philadelphia, PA**

The recently designed 3400 sq. ft. flagship for Comcast's products and services is truly a "Shop of the Future" as designed by Charles E. Broudy & Assoc. of Philadelphia, PA. This high-tech showcase is a one-stop shopping location that gives shoppers a "glimpse into the communications, information and entertainment world of tomorrow."

The visitor enters the shop through a fiber optic archway and once inside there is a full presentation of Comcast's cable, cellular and paging services, or the shopper can subscribe to Primestar direct-to-home satellite TV, or get upgrades on the latest in local events via the Comcast @ Home Cable network.

Stainless steel and glass elliptical tables, outfitted with laptop P.O.P. stations "orbit within a pathway of arches" that lead the shoppers to the rear of the space. Here a dramatic nine screen video wall—seen from the entrance—continually runs highlights of Comcast's offerings and other information stations. The dark floor and ceiling plus the arcade of stainless steel arches that create a dynamic arcade pattern through the length of the store add to the fun and excitement of the space.

The interior is dramatically illuminated with theatrical lighting fixtures with barn door housings to direct the light. The side walls which also seem to bow—and continue the rhythm of the arches—carry product display and information in the form of colorful graphics and lifestyle photography. "Prominent fixturing and billboard style 3M graphics grace the perimeter wall with theatrical presence." All the lights, sound, video, computers, store openings and closings and special evening programs are choreographed by a master computer operated via a touch screen podium and a wireless remote control: a truly high tech approach for a store promoting technology for today and tomorrow.

Screenz Digital Universe

Clark St., Chicago, IL

Design: **Johnson Design Group, Park Ridge, IL**

Principal: **Mark Johnson**

Designers: **Matt Wylier & Jesus Herreras**

Colors & Materials: **Cynthia Passarelli**

For Screenz Digital: **Dir. of Visual Marketing & Retail Planning: Randy Sattler**

Architecture: **Chipman/Adams, Chicago, IL**

Graphics: **Mark Kostabi**

Photography: **John Shelves, Summit Studio, Chicago, IL**

For those of you who want to get "wet" and "surf the net" but haven't tried it yet, the solution is at Screenz Digital Universe. At Screenz, the visitor pays by the minute with a Screenz Smart Card to access the Internet, explore a library of CD Rom entertainment titles as well as "entertainment" applications, conduct on-line research or produce professional work while away from home or office. It is a "try it—you'll like it" approach to the latest in PC technology.

For the novice, Screenz provide a simple graphic user interface which makes "navigation" easy. There are full time "explorer guides," an interactive help system and on-site Help Desk available to direct users and "lead them along their journey."

The award-winning design is "non-intimidating and comfortable" and it was designed by the Johnson Design Group to make computers a social experience accessible to everyone from novice to advanced practitioner. Mark Johnson, principal of the design firm, said, "We look a very rectangular space and softened it through the use of a curved soffit and aisle scheme. The combination of hard surfaces in high traffic areas and a soft, curved carpet pattern leads the customer through the space."

A smart and up-to-the-moment urban "neighborhood environment" was created up front by the use of

brick, wood and metal played against a variety of bright, clear colors and a "wild magnetic menu board." The Coffee Bar is located here and it has been designed to be the center of activity for the store providing services, information, merchandise and refreshments."

The designers created a flexible festering system which allows for single unit stations, as well as two and four person stations. The Cyberbar area is planned as a quiet place where cyber citizens can have a degree of privacy. Internet classes can be conducted at the rear of the store.

Adding to the fun and excitement of the space are the colorful and stimulating graphics created by Mark Kostabi.

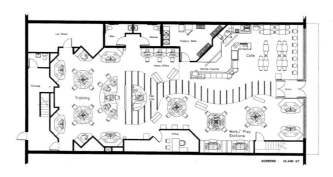

Digital

**Comdex Trade Show,
Minneapolis, MN**

Design: **Shea Architects, Minneapolis, MN**

Architect: **Larsen Design Group**

Photography: **Sinclair Reinsch**

Digital Equipment Corp. created an OEM Storage division to market their data storage products and the parent company asked Shea Architects and the Larsen Design Group to create an exciting, energizing, and entertaining display for the identity and recognition of the new storage division. The display/exhibit would be introduced at a Comdex show; the computer industry's most important venue. Here a product line needs a unique identity because it affects the merchandise acceptance later on in the marketplace. Since the Comdex audience is a sophisticated one—mostly top level managers and computer engineers—a multi-layered approach was used to create "visual intrigue" in a museum-like setting.

The overall visual approach was developed to represent each of the three product areas in the marketing literature and in the exhibit. The icons that were developed include a circle for disk drives; a nine square pattern for solid drives and a circle within a square for tape drives. Each icon was selected because of the physical properties of the product. The exhibit area was divided into six major pods and the three products each had a pod to itself. The designers selected clever, amusing and memorable "analogies" to represent the products.

Storage items such as refrigerators and luggage represent the storage capabilities of the disk drives. Concorde jet nose cones illustrate the speed of solid state drives and to illustrate the large volume storage capabilities of the tape drives, a tower of toppling books and tall library shelves were used.

Instead of a dull and traditional approach this entertaining and more unusual presentation of product and company image proved very effective. To further the "good times" feeling, the designers also came up with giveaways such as tee shirts, bags, coffee mugs, literature, etc.

A portion of a giant globe hung over the exhibit to emphasize Digital's global nature and also to create a strong vertical presence at the show. The registration desk with a built-in large OEM storage identity filled one of the areas as did a conference space. "All elements were designed to reflect the unique and progressive image the client needed to portray"—and entertain the serious buyer as well.

Microsoft USA

Concord, CA

Design: **Retail Planning Associates, Columbus, OH**

CEO/Chairman: **Doug Cheeseman**

Account Executive: **Michael Bills, V.P.**

Project Director: **Linda Rosine, V.P.**

Associate Project Director: **Laura Evans**

Retail Strategist: **Edd Johns**

Environmental Designer: **Conrad Chin**

Merchandiser: **Vince Notaroberto**

Visual Communications: **Tim Smith, V.P./Adam Limbach**

Photography: **Michael Houton, Columbus, OH**

The 500 sq. ft. prototype design store, created by Retail Planning Associates for the Microsoft Company, is focused on providing access to Microsoft's software as well as providing insights into the products' features, utilities and abilities to perform.

Information is delivered via interactive means as part of the overall Visual Communications hierarchy, and electronic as well as traditional paper based communication guide the customers through the purchasing experience.

The system of floor and wall fixtures, the customer communication graphics, and the interaction devices were all designed to "enhance the presentation and accessibility of Microsoft's products." Since the fixtures are all modular in concept, they can be adapted to a variety of store types, sizes and formats and also product mixes.

Two interactive stations and two TV monitors allow the shoppers to interact with the many Microsoft product demonstrations and advertisements. In the 500 sq. ft. prototype there is a full range of products displayed with 300 facing (rather than spine showing) and over 1000 total units.

To increase the sense of space, the floor is patterned in bands of light and dark woods and panels of light wood back up some of the face-out, modular wall fixtures. The

floor fixtures are high-tech in concept and in materials and they ride on big casters so that the floor arrangement can readily be changed. The units are interactive in that shoppers "communicate" with them and the design allows for face-out merchandise presentation. The lighting in the store combines dropped halogen fixtures with incandescent track lighting on the perimeter wall merchandising display.

The shop was designed to be self-standing or it can be adapted to appear as a shop-within-a-shop in computer stores, book stores, department stores—or even in supermarkets in Europe where software is often available.

The 10,000 sq. ft. warehouse concept store was designed by Crabtree Hall/ Plan Creatif Group for the Maplen Stores Group of the United Kingdom. The client previously marketed their components through catalogs, and this store—designed to have the widest possible consumer appeal— is aimed at "the hobbyist, the educationalist, computer 'nerd,' and the electronics wizard."

In order to reinforce the "catalog's action packed pages," the store is clearly segregated into areas that cater to specific interests. The clear supporting graphics help the shopper to find and select the products and specialists with technical advise are available at the service desks located throughout the store. An exposed mezzanine deck runs the length of one wall and contains the 15,000 components that make up the Serviced Components Store that is a key element in the Mondo operation. In addition, interactive displays and live product demonstrations are "an essential part of Mondo's buzz" and they add to the sense of entertainment in the space. Another entertaining feature is the Network Cafe where "students can meet and browse the latest technical publications as they 'surf the net.'"

Color, light, and graphics combine to create a feeling of fun and fantasy in the giant warehouse setting where the ceiling has been painted a dark color and the floor and walls are a basic light gray color. Color-filled friezes and even full walls are brightly accented in color to highlight specific areas. Even the hanging fluorescent fixtures are painted in assorted vibrant colors.

"Mondo has been designed to enable the retailer to rapidly reflect the constantly evolving "World of Electronics & Beyond"; it's highly adaptable store layout and engineered to stimulate the senses of both visual and aural at every opportunity."

Mondo

Leeds, England

Design: **Crabtree Hall/Plan Creatif Group, London, England**

Partner in Charge: **David Mackay**

Photography: **Jon O'Brien**

Ultimate Electronics

Tulsa, OK

Design: **Design Forum, Dayton, OH**

V.P., Project Designer: **Scott Smith**

V.P., Project Architect: **Ralph Wolfe**

Photography: **Jamie Padgett, Chicago, IL**

Ultimate Electronics prides itself on the vast array of products it carries: from DSS technology to car stereos to walkmans and subwoofers. In creating this new big-box retail outlet, Ultimate Electronics, with the help of Design Forum of Dayton, OH, hoped to convey the chain's outstanding service and also make a powerful statement that tells shoppers that this is a great place to shop. The company also hoped to solidify its position as the "premiere, high-end, electronic specialist in the western U.S."

To get around in the large, warehouse type structure, there are light box departmental focals and "fluid category signage" that empower the shoppers to find and make their own selections though assistance is available if needed. The firm's integrated, high-tech AV systems serve as the main centerpiece in the Planning Center and Home Theater areas. In the former area, educational signage and graphics inform the shopper about the key product attributes and the interior signage system also communicates store amenities and services that reinforce Ultimate's professional image in the marketplace.

Though the setting is basically neutral in color, it is highlighted and accentuated with brightly-colored signage and areas of warm, natural wood. Curved valances, soffits and service desks tend to soften the look of the retail space under the dark painted ceiling into which fluorescent fixtures have been recessed. Some areas are further enhanced with track lighting. The overall effect is more upscaled and sophisticated than one would expect in what—from the outside—looks like a big box store set along a highway.

Moby-Dick

"Huzza! huzza!" cried the seamen, as with swinging tarpaulins they hailed the act of nailing the gold to the mast.

"It's a white whale, I say," resumed Ahab, as he threw down the top-maul: "a white whale. Skin your eyes for him, men; look sharp for white water; if ye see but a bubble, sing out."

"Captain Ahab," said Tashtego, "That white whale must be the same that some call Moby-Dick."

MELVILLE

Treasure

I now felt for the
of exploration. Th
habited; my ship
behind, and nothi
of me but dumb
I turned hither an
the trees. Here
flowering plants,
here and there I
one raised his he
of rock and hiss
noise not unlike
a top. Little di
he was a deadly
the noise was th

STEV

Souvenirs

and

time the joy
sle was unin-
tes I had left
lived in front
es and fowls.
hither among
d there were
known to me;
snakes, and
from a ledge
at me with a
spinning of
suppose that
my, and that
amous rattle.

ON

20,000 Leagues Under the Sea

Various kinds of isis, cluster
of pure tuft-coral, prickly fungi,
and anemones, formed a
brilliant garden of flowers,
enamelled with porphitae,
decked with their collarettes
of blue tentacles, sea-stars stud-
ding the sandy bottom, together
with asterophytons like fine lace
embroidered by the hands of
naiads, whose festoon were
waved by the gentle undula-
tions caused by our walk,

VERNE

Warner Bros. Studio Store

New York, NY

Design: **Jon Greenberg Assoc., Southfield, MI**

For JGA:

Design Team: **Kenneth Nisch, June Lester, Mike O'Neill, Jon Ebersole, Renae Hawley**

For Warner Bros:

Studio Store: **Dan Romanelli, Peter Starrett, Dennis Adomaitis, Kathy Prost, Terron Schaefer, Audrey Schlaepfer, Karine Joret, Michele Patton, Steve Runyon, Tom Sandonato, Marcia Tabler**

Murals and Accessories: **Warner Bros. Scenic Art Dept.**

Children's Interactive Display: **Penwal Industries, CA**

With the Warner Bros. Studio store, nine stories high, impressively situated on 57th Street, this fabled street has become the entertainment hub of NYC. With neighbors such as Nike just across the street and a variety of noted theme restaurants just up the street—this is where the action is.

In October 1993 the Fifth Ave. store opened with 30,000 sq. ft. on three levels. Just three years later it has expanded to 75,000 sq. ft. of retail entertainment on nine floors filled with fun, games, souvenirs, art, and so much to see, sample and buy.

Peter Starrett, President of Warner Bros. Studio Stores said, "By combining traditional retail and a cafe with interactive games with a 3-D film—all within a highly themed environment, we hope to set a new world standard with the New York flagship for what retail entertainment is all about."

Every floor is themed with the Looney Tune cartoon characters and the merchandise on view. The main level is merchandised with souvenirs linked to the latest Warner Bros. theatrical and feature animation films. Here there are the New York, NY shop and the WB Classics area as well as multi-media towers, TV monitors, familiar cartoon characters looking down from the trompe l'oeil ceiling—and this is where the adventure begins.

On the second floor, also filled with N.Y. icons, there is upscaled adult merchandise as well as Daffy Duck as a cab driver and giant sculptures of Superman, Batman and Wonder Woman. The N.Y. theme continues with a visit to the American Museum of Natural History and the Flintstones.

Bugs Bunny is at the wheel as visitors to the third level continue their tour of N.Y. under a ceiling that ripples with stars and stripes. The tour boat covers giftware, sports apparel at the WB Sports shop, and housewares.

All sorts of amenities and customer conveniences are available on the fourth floor where tickets are sold for the 3-D adventures of Marvin the Martian. A new Gallery on five—the home of animation art, contemporary art and fine arts—is a shop within a shop. The collection is constantly evolving and the diversified art covers a vast price range. "From original animation art to contemporary sculpture and distinctive gifts, the range of art options available through the Gallery is simply unparalleled." Adjacent to the Gallery is the Moving Picture Cafe where families can enjoy a dining experience in a theme related ambience.

The sixth and seventh levels are devoted to children and infants. The Wacky Acme Lab is filled with loads of hands-on, interactive games and activities and the neighboring Wacky Acme Candy Co. carries 130 kinds of candy in bulk. Carrying through the "lab" concept, the ceiling has Looney Tune characters dressed up as scientists while other characters on the floor serve as guides. Children's apparel is void on both levels and there are toys and games and a coloring station on seven.

Up on the eighth floor is Marvin the Martian's theme shop. In a specially designed 74 seat theater visitors can meet Marvin as he adventures into the third dimension in the first computer animated 3-D film. Of course, classic cartoon characters are also there to see him on his way.

A large room fills more of the ninth floor and it can be rented for receptions, birthday parties, etc. It, too, is filled with murals, theme and excitement. Other unique features include a nine story glass elevator that seems to be powered by a life size Superman and a five story wall sculpture "Looney Tunes & Friends Meet N.Y." The kids will be sure to want to see the heroic sized Bugs Bunny doing his Statue of Liberty impersonation on four.

Summing it up: "A premier entertainment shopping experience combining interactive displays, dramatic multi media environs, and a diverse assortment of high quality, exclusively designed merchandise inspired by the glamour and excitement of the entertainment industry."

Universal
Studio Store

Universal Studios, Hollywood, CA

Design: **Universal Creative, Universal Studio Recreation, Universal City, CA**

Director of Design: **Bob Hale**

Project Architect: **Mark Lescaut**

Graphics Manager: **Mark Hellier**

Interior Design: **Judy Van Wyk**

For Universal Studio Recreation Mdse Group, Orlando, FL

Sr. V.P.: **John Ball**

Mgr. Store Design & Visual Merchandising: **Jeff Fisher**

For Gensler & assoc., Pasadena, CA

Project Principal: **Bruce Campbell**

Design Director: **Robert Green**

Design: **Jeff Henry**

Film and film-making are the focus of the 6200 sq. ft. retail store that has become a great added attraction for tourists to the Universal Studios in Hollywood. The store salutes Universal's history and its contributions to the movie-making industry.

"Welcome to our Universe" greets the tourist approaching the store and a geometric blue and white terrazzo design is set before the three entrances into the store. "Smile—you are on camera": a camera crane juts out from the ceiling with a stylized director and camera operator behind a Panavision camera. Shoppers get the feeling that they are being filmed. In contrast to the new technology, there is also a camera and camera dolly such as those used in the Silent Era with a director with a bull horn behind the camera— shooting the next scene.

Inside, the ceiling is high—14 ft. up—and it is painted white up front and the exposed trusses and HVAC systems, further back, are painted midnight blue. Throughout the store there is a mix of metal and wood. The floors are maple wood and maple panels are interspersed with white ones along the walls for accent and

impact. There is a stainless steel and black theater marquee over a video wall and the cash/wrap counter is color blocked in gray and black. The floor fixtures are brushed aluminum accented with rose/gold, ribbed metal. The wall units are built on the same module as the floor fixtures for ease of product presentation and flexibility and also keeps the shelf and hardware consistent throughout.

Framed in black and stainless steel is the large seamless video wall—strategically placed—where by means of a custom laser disc—

highlights of Universal's past and present, in the form of trailers for upcoming movies, entertains shoppers in the store. The fluid, color blocked design of the cash/wrap allows for the use of stylized graphics of famous stars and celebrities of Universal's firmament.

"We have created a showcase store for our best product groups and the Universal Studios Hollywood experience is not complete till you shop at this flagship location."

Jurassic Park Retail Store

Universal Studios, Hollywood, CA

Design: **AAD, Phoenix, AZ**

Principal: **Mike Stevenson AAD**
Universal Creative, Universal Studios Recreation,
Universal City, CA

Project Director: **David Wilson**

Project Manager: **Bob Garrison**

Project Architect: **Craig Doyle**

Graphics Manager: **Mark Hellier**
Universal Studios Recreation Merchandise
Group, Orlando, FL

Sr. VP: **John Ball**

VP: **Marcie Kay**

Mgr Store Design/Visual Merchandising: **Jeff Fisher**

Following the success of the feature film Jurassic Park, Universal Studios Hollywood commissioned AAD (Associates in Architecture & Design) of Phoenix to design a retail and restaurant environment to capitalize on the success of the film—and its sequel. The highly themed 4800 sq. ft. space is the "exit store" for the Jurassic Park themed adventure ride.

Through the use of colors, materials and textures, the designers created a space with "fossilized" walls, heavy "stone" floors, earthy colors and the luxurious overgrown feeling of a jungle. They also expanded the thematic elements that related to the movie. The scaled down jeep holds multiple apparel SKUs, the raptor bone pedestal is a focal point for the apparel area and the high-ticket items are securely displayed in the dinosaur egg incubator. Plush animals find their perfect habitat in the leafy foliage of the jungle tree. There is even an appearance by Mr. DNA. The store is a "sequence of themes and props that draw the shopper from merchandise display to merchandise display.

According to Jeff Fisher, Mgr of Store Design & Visual Merchandising for Universal Studios, "It was the first time we exited the attraction directly into the retail store to create the ultimately seamless experience. This concept generated an incredible revenue for us. AAD truly succeeded on this project."

Viacom Entertainment Store

Chicago, IL

Design: **FRCH Worldwide Design Int'l., New York, NY**

Photography: **Dan Forer, Forer Inc., Miami, FL**

Making a big, bright and colorful splash on North Michigan Ave. in Chicago—a street already glistening with retail entertainment—is the new Viacom concept store. The 30,000 sq. ft., two-level store features exclusive merchandise with displays, museum quality artifacts and memorabilia, live entertainment and assorted interactive activities.

Summer M. Redstone, Chairman and CEO of Viacom, Inc. said, "The Viacom Entertainment Store is more than a store. It is a brand showcase. That raises the bar on entertainment retailing and redefines the shopping experience for every generation of consumer. This store offers something for everyone in the family." To create the "most engaging retail environment anywhere," Viacom called upon the most innovative and talented

entertainment producers and marketers as well as the design talents of FRCH Worldwide Design of New York. The Viacom Entertainment Stores is a direct link to MTV, VH-1, Nickelodeon, Nick at Nite, Paramount Pictures and Star Trek.

The space was conceived as a giant "shell" with wide open floor space and soaring ceilings. The store's design is flexible and each branded area can be changed and/or updated to effectively display new products as they are produced and released. The merchandise is shown in individual branded "boutiques" with special effects and ambiences. The merchandise found in the Nickelodeon shop was developed from a "kid's point of view" and incorporates the irreverence that permeates both the network and the shows on

it. The Ultimate Room is Nickelodeon's on-air sweepstakes, and the product line that is presented here includes a bed with cubby holes where kids can hide their "stuff" as well as other strange, funny and even weird pieces of furniture or furnishings.

In Nick at Nite shoppers will find a line of clothing, sleepwear, jewelry, collectibles and other items featuring photography of classic episodes of the I Love Lucy TV series along with the "heart" logo and Lucy's signature. Also available is dinnerware and novelty apparel with the Club Babalu logo, the club where Ricky Ricardo performed.

For the MTV audience there are three lines of apparel based on the characters Abducted, Rave Girl and Alien. These are inspired by Japanese animae, girl bands and extraterrestrials.

The popular Star Trek Gallery contains an assortment of authentic and replicas of props, masks, starships and memorabilia signed by the Star Trek actors, "antique" licensed toys and original, signed and numbered lithographs.

The Paramount Back Lot is merchandised with sportswear branded "crew" or "actor." In addition to the regularly scheduled events which include musical performances, readings and celebrity appearances and

the 70-seat cafe called Station Break, there are over 30 interactive stations and a variety of multimedia. The interactive stations are called "experiential hooks" and they are fun stops that are both high and low tech. One can be transported from the Starship Enterprise via green-screen technology—and even get a photo taken of the space adventure. Kids can peep through real periscopes located in Nickelodeon's Hideout Hut and "spy" on what's going on around the store. For MTV fans there is a Rant Room where they are free to "sound off."

Viacom expects to open another three or four flagship brand building stores in key U.S. cities and then possibly franchise in major international markets.

Go Overboard

Shedd Aquarium, Chicago, IL

Associate Architect Retail Design: **Schwartz Architects, New York, NY**

Principal in Charge: **Frederic Schwartz, AIA**

Associate in Charge: **Paul Cali**

Senior Project Designer: **Leslie Y. Ghym**

Project Team: **Bruno Arnold/Shane Braddock/Steven Petrides**

The Shedd Aquarium Design & Planning Teams

Architect: **Esherick Homesy Dodge & Davis (EHDD), Chicago, IL**

Principal in Charge: **Charles M. Davis, AIA**

Project Designer/Manager: **Marc L'Italien, AIA**

Project Architect: **Pierre Zetterberg**

Design Team: **Kim Sqanson/Amy Storek/Orla Huq/Glennis Briggs**

Consultants: **Light: Schuler & Shooks, Inc.**

Graphic Design: **Alex Isley, Shedd Aquarium, Graphics Dept.**

Photography: **Doug Snower Photography**

A new and delightful experience has debuted in the John G. Shedd Aquarium in Chicago. It is the exciting and unique 5000 sq. ft. underwater-like shopping adventure called Go Overboard. Aquatic related and Shedd branded products are sold here.

The design challenge presented to the architects/designers by Ted A. Beattie, president and CEO of the Aquarium, was—"We wanted coming into the store to feel like diving into the ocean. By creating a lively setting where shoppers can learn about all types of aquatic life, we help people better understand and appreciate the ocean and its marvelous sea creatures."

There's an underwater feeling throughout the store. To create the "watery illusion," the design combines theatrical lighting by six specially designed water effect projectors, 50 surround-sound speakers, water patterned carpeting and the unique easy to follow and shop floor plan. Adding to the "submerged" ambience are the video wall and the seven underseas photo murals. Suspended from the ceiling as the centerpiece of the design is the 1400 pound gigantic octopus. It stretches 28 ft. across and ten feet high, and each of the eight ten-foot-long tentacles is wrapped around the building's original circular foundation

columns. The eyes are TV monitors that continually show myriad animal and human eyes. Ten other, larger-than-life, sea creatures float over the five departments in the multi-faceted specialty store. They include a leopard shark, a green sea turtle and a golden eel.

The largest area in the store is the children's department which is located directly below the ominous octopus. Other areas are themed such as the Coral Reef and the Rain Forest and there is even a Book area for grown-ups.

"From the design to the merchandise to the staff, every aspect of the store has been created to be an exciting, fun and extraordinary retailing experience. We want guests to feel immersed in a water world of adventure where they can get items that are difficult, if not impossible, to find anywhere else. There is nothing ordinary about Go Overboard," said Christina Gunn, Director of Merchandising.

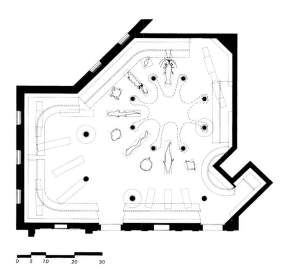

Science Fiction Zone

Las Vegas Hilton, Las Vegas, NV

In this fantasy land where Theme is king, a new Spacequest Casino is scheduled to appear in the Las Vegas Hilton which is already home to the roller skating odyssey *Starlight Express*. In preparation for the new arrival, Science Fiction Zone was recently unwrapped as an "attention getting gift shop" which will complement the casino and the skating spectacle.

According to the designers, Schafer Associates, the "draw is the entertainment and excitement that is promised and fulfilled with the vibrant light, the sound and the many interactive features." Adding to the draw—and the "cosmic ambience"—is the fiber optic floor that cuts out into the hotel corridor at the shop's front door. It brings the energy and vitality out to the traffic. The Science Fiction Zone logo is embedded in the middle of the floor and a light source, behind the cash/wrap, causes the "O" in "Zone" to glow; the circumference of the circle slowly turns to yellow—blends to purple—then reveals the whole logo.

Meanwhile "stars" twinkle in the background of the circle. The store itself has "a dark, alluring cavernous feel." Adding to the store's futuristic ambience are the metallic cable perimeter wall system and fixtures, and the custom designed expanding metal suspended ceiling treatment, and the incandescent track lighting. S.F.Z's kinetic ambience was designed as part of an overall strategic program which layers prototypical Hilton gift shop concepts with atmospheric and theme associated components. Metallic finishes, a signature blueberry color and the "O" icon all make S.F.Z. different.

The product mix contained in the 635 sq. ft. space is all fun and entertainment, and capitalizes on the popularity of The X-Files, Star Trek, Star Wars, Independence Day and other sci-fi movies, TV shows and books. There are space models, science projects, and glow-in-the-dark stars as well as robots, "aliens," mugs, caps, tee shirts and other out-of-this-world memorabilia.

The result is an efficient and economical store that supports Hilton's standards, enhances brand identification and ensures operational efficiency while providing a sense of entertainment.

Design: **Schafer Associates, Oakbrook Terrace, IL**

Project Architect: **Design Core, Las Vegas, NV**

Photographer: **Bob Briskey, Briskey Photography, Hinsdale, IL**

Awesome Atom's Science Store

Arizona Science Center, Phoenix, AZ

Design: **Miller/Rausch, Phoenix, AZ**

Photography: **Dave Tevis, Tevis Photographic, Tempe, AZ**

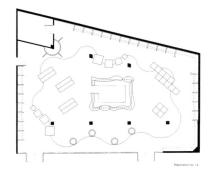

Working with the Delstar Group that specializes in unique retail stores and gift shops, the Miller/Rausch design firm in Phoenix, AZ came up with the design concept for the Awesome Atom's Science store. The concept was realized in a 2770 sq. ft. space in the Arizona Science Center in downtown Phoenix.

"At Awesome Atom's, we eschewed the norms of museum store design," said Julie Vitiello Swanson of the Miller/Rausch firm, "and worked to create a retail area that in and of itself draws people in, yet once inside exudes the same hands-on philosophy of the Service Center. We designed Awesome Atom's to be a place where patrons would feel compelled and comfortable to explore and play with an amazing array of hard-to-find, educational—yet entertaining—items."

The concrete building beams, columns, and building systems remain visible in the store's design. Also left exposed—"to enhance the science learning experience"—are the plumbing, electrical and mechanical systems. They are identified by signage that explain the inner workings of the building. The conduit leading to the lighting down the center spine of the store is swagged in rhythm to accentuate the exposed systems.

36 in. wide perimeter display units are organized around the large amoeba-shaped carpet patterned with space motifs. These units are framed by colored and curved plexi-glass panels that carry the signage. "Light-piping" causes the plexi edges to appear to be edge lit. A scale model rocket with flashing lights, smoking engines and glowing fluorescent interior workings serves as the focal point for the space. A source of surprise and wonderment is the floating astronaut caught in the gentle glow of a dimly lit area. The designers used bold fluorescent colored plexi-glass and displayers to create the various geometric forms that give the space its character.

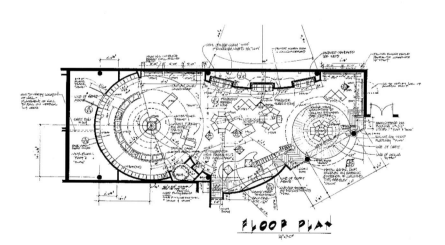

FLOOR PLAN

Adjacent to the casino floor of the Hard Rock Hotel/Casino in Las Vegas is the first ever, retail store designed as a complete, self-standing unit. It is a 2000 sq. ft. emporium selling unique merchandise—all with the Hard Rock Hotel logo or name.

The store was designed by JGA (Jon Greenberg & Assoc.) of Southfield, MI, working with Warwick Stone who is responsible as the Create Director of HRH for the interior and exterior design of the hotel/casino including the famous guitar sign. "In its no-nonsense approach to the world of rock and roll, the Hard Rock Hotel retail store treats the shoppers to a unique shopping experience. It celebrates the guitar in all its rock and roll glory "and encases the varied products in a setting that includes an exposed ceiling and industrial and distressed finishes.

The store's entrance is flanked by patina brass columns and it is illuminated by a glowing dome. From that corner entrance, the wood floor is designed to be "reminiscent of the starburst gradient of a wood guitar." The logo-ed merchandise is displayed on custom, raw metal, industrial style fixtures on casters for easy mobility in this ever changing world.

Adding to the rebellious "rock and roll image" is the authentic motorcycle parked atop one of the massive merchandise fixtures near the cash/wrap counter. "From mannequin bodies with guitar neck 'heads'—to the instrument cases on wheels used as flexible fixtures—the store has a true industrial/contemporary feel."

Hard Rock Retail Store

Hard Rock Hotel/Casino, Las Vegas, NV

Design: **JGA, Southfield, MI**

Account Executive: **Kenneth Nisch**

Creative Director: **Jenness Anderson**

Senior Designer: **Michael Benincasa**

Creative Resources: **Renae Hawley**

Design Consultant for Hard Rock Hotel/Casino: **Warwick Stone**

Complementing the wood guitars that are on display throughout the store is the herringbone patterned wood floor. Another "work of art" and gasp-producer is the guitar shaped cash/wrap which was designed to be a gigantic Fender guitar.

A central focal fixture with light and animation draws curious shoppers to the rear of the store. A light column designed and constructed by Larry Albright and Assoc. of Venice, CA "ignites the area with a light show" in front of the tremendous T-shirt wall. The column is a hollow acrylic tube filled with bits of color. When the bits are "energized with electricity" they create "bolts of lightning through the tube."

Nobody seems to leave the Hard Rock Hotel retail store without some small souvenir of the shopping experience.

Planet
Hollywood
Retail Store

Woodfield Mall, Schaumburg, IL

Design: **Pompei,AD, New York, NY**

Design Principal: **Ron Pompei**

Project Manager: **Nick Arauz**

Design Team: **Ostap Rudekyavich & Cal Petrescu**

For Planet Hollywood:
President/CEO: **Robert Earl**

VP of Development: **John McCann**

Director of Retail: **Sandi Chriqui**

Photography: **Scott McDonald**

All the pizzazz of Planet Hollywood and none of the food! For movie buffs and film fans who love the Hollywood of past and present and who would rather buy their memories than eat them, Planet Hollywood Retail shops are now appearing as independent stores in malls. According to Robert Earl, the founder and president of Planet Hollywood, "We have been pleasantly surprised with the reaction to this new line of merchandise and the new concept." The line offered in the stand alone locations have small logo identification and features product not offered in the restaurants.

Pompei,AD, a New York based design firm, created this 3000 sq. ft. retail store in the upscaled Woodfield Mall in Schaumburg, IL, which is close to Chicago. The designers filled the space to capacity with icons and images of Hollywood's heydays. The shopper passes through an entrance "gateway" reminiscent of the florid flourishes that overwhelmed the old Paramount Studio gates. The shopper then steps into an eternal night where a mural of night-time L.A. on the perimeter walls creates the first impact. The dazzling effect is created by using fluorescent set paint and hidden back lights.

Other backlit "buildings" or "flats"—such as one would find on a sound stage—appear in front of the mural. "The fixtures are deliberately designed to look like facades or stage flats to reinforce the theatrical design fee," said Ron Pompei. Memorable film moments are captured on the TV monitors which fill some of the "open windows."

The flooring looks like asphalt and goes with the backlot theme. A huge filmstrip runs overhead and leads from the entrance to the rear wall where the strip actually originates from a huge camera lens. The lens is fitted with a TV monitor. As the strip unreels across the dark ceiling that is filled with pin spots that suggest the light streaked sky at a film premier, faces of stars of the golden screen are seen on the swooping film strip.

Like the simple, clean wood and metal wall fixtures, the floor fixtures also display hard and soft goods. The orange colored fixtures stand out from the asphalt simulated floor with the famous hand and footprints "embedded" in it. "We used forced perspective that defies the original geometry of the long, rectangular shape of the lease space.

In addition to the swooping and sweeping, face-filled filmstrip, a collage of Hollywood memorabilia contributes to the "I Love Movies" ambience. Oversized artifacts of the actual merchandise also reinforce the concept. Illuminating Concepts, the company responsible for the fabulous lighting plan, also programmed lights to move from the giant replicas to the products they represent.

Thus, "using theatrical lighting techniques and movie-inspired special effects, the design captures the Hollywood mystique and brings the merchandise to life."

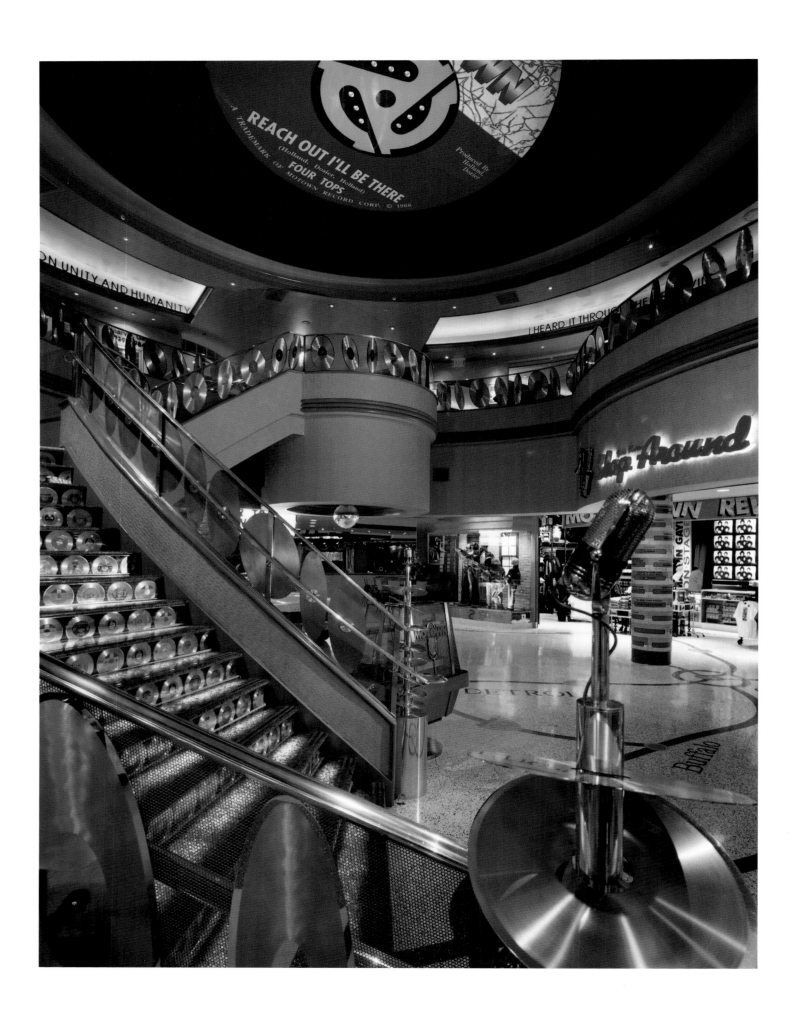

Motown

Las Vegas, NE &
New York, NY

Design: **Haverson Architects and Designers, Greenwich, CT**

Photography: **Paul Warchol**

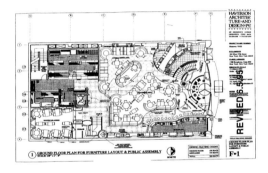

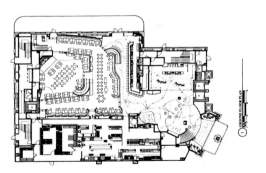

To get into the always "hot"—always hectic and crammed full and crowded Motown Cafe in Las Vegas—in the New York New York hotel/casino complex—you have to stop and shop the retail store. It is conveniently located up front. Dramatic show windows with icons of the recording industry as well as the fashions being offered in the retail store are part of the pulsating energy up front

The shop is set back somewhat under the overhanging mezzanine and just opposite the stunning brass/glass and grid stairway ornamented with brushed silver and gold "records." In contrast to this opulence, the retail shop is like a little bit of very urban New York with its simulated brick walls, posters and graphics. On the terrazzo floor patterned with routes to be traveled, are the industrial black grid systems combined with exposed theatrical lighting. All the fixtures are industrial in style: big, black and riding high on sturdy casters.

The multi-level display table under the red welcoming banner that spans the opening suggests a theatrical trunk or instrument mover all black and edged in metal. The rear wall brings the swinging action of the themed restaurant into the retail store where on a video wall made up of 16 monitors—it's always showtime!

Rich cherry colored wood, black trim and black terrazzo tiles create a contrast to the merchandise in "Shop Around," the two-story retail shop in the Motown on E. 57th St. in New York City. Shoppers can enter from the main waiting room near the entrance or directly through a double door on the street. The art deco heritage of the building that formerly housed a Horn & Hardart Automat appears in the gentle bowed walls and the repetitive use of moldings. TV screens, built into the rear merchandising wall, and back-lit colored graphics add some sparkle to the comfortably-illuminated setting.

Planet Hollywood

Walt Disney World, Orlando, FL

Design: **The Rockwell Group, New York, NY**

Photography: **Paul Warchol**

No theme restaurant is complete without one, and from many reports, no theme restaurant can do without one. The "one" is usually located at the entrance or very near it, and it is the souvenir or retail shop where branded and logo emblazoned merchandise can be found. It extends the visit, it provides the tangible proof that you were there, and it produces a tremendous amount of revenue for the restaurant. The shops usually follow through on the look and theme of the restaurant and often the merchandise is kept behind a counter so that salespeople can control the action, especially when the shop gets crowded.

Here is the retail area in the Planet Hollywood in Orlando, FL. Designed by Rockwell Group of New York who has designed over 20 Planet Hollywoods, the shop in the 30,000 sq. ft. restaurant continues the movie experience in the angled, multi-paneled, multi-media crown that makes a dynamic sweep over the bowed service counter. The red finished shelved wall behind the counter follows the same semi-circular design and the products shown here are illuminated by many MR16 halide lamps set on the undersurface of the "entertainment" loaded crown.

CBS Retail Store

New York, NY

Design: **The Rockwell Group, New York, NY**

The client, CBS (Columbia Broadcasting System) commissioned the Rockwell Group to design a prototype retail store in a 300 sq. ft. space. The client wanted "a memorable space" that would sell a variety of branded retail goods.

The design concept came from "mixed past and present images" of CBS history with icons of the Golden Age of Television such as Jackie Gleason and Lucille Ball as well as current stars such as David Letterman.

The small store is located next to the entrance to the "Late Night with David Letterman" show at the Ed Sullivan Theater on Broadway— which is also the home of the popular TV/Radio themed restaurant, Sullivan's. "We've designed the exterior of the store with TVs embedded on the sidewalk so people waiting on line to get into the Letterman show can watch and shop." Inside the colorfully furnished store with its elliptical plan are giant photo blow-ups of the TV stars, video monitors replaying highlights of great shows and an assortment of T-shirts, sweats, tote bags, jackets, caps, a CBS teddy bear, mugs and other branded or logo-ed memorabilia.

Official All Star Cafe Retail Shop

New York, NY

Design: **The Rockwell Group, New York, NY**

"The Official All Star Cafe is a rich, fun-filled sports environment" that provides patrons with a visceral sense of being there. Some areas in the 20,000 sq. ft. arena-like interior are set aside for shops or counters where sports related souvenirs and All Star logo merchandise is sold. Like the restaurant, they are also a celebration of sports and sporting events.

Located near the entrance and where diners wait to be seated, is the main retail area. It is set behind an undulating guard rail of ocher yellow grid and galvanized metal piping. Just beyond it is the back of the curving sales counter. A dark blue carpeted aisle separates the service desk from the perimeter wall which is cubbyholed and filled with folded and stacked garments. Above the merchandise is a sweeping frieze that combines shadow box displays with panels for the pin-up displays of merchandise.

The flooring consists of radiating bands of red and yellow carpeting that seems to sweep the visitor into the shop. The counters are red aniline dyed wood trimmed with black and white striped field posts capped by red truss arches decorated with the logo "A." Over this recessed shop are some giant video monitors that add to the excitement of the place.

Also shown is a secondary shop—for those who may have missed the main one.

It is a draw as to which is the greater attraction in this dynamic and exciting family restaurant/retail environment. Is it the food served in the tropical rain forest setting under giant mushrooms and surrounded by animated butterflies, crocodiles, snakes, elephants and gorillas in the make-believe jungle, or is it the wonderland of colorful and lovable plush animals and other ecology-oriented and logo-branded merchandise?

Besides the T-shirts, sweats, caps, stuffed animals and toys, there is also a pet shop where exotic toucans, macaws or cockatoos can be purchased.

If you look past the crocodile-filled moat and beyond the brightly-plummaged tropical birds suspended amid the bunches of bananas and other jungle fruits—under a ceiling lost in foliage—there is a large gift shop that is as imaginative, adventure filled and as entertaining as the dining experience around it.

Rainforest Cafe

Disney Village Marketplace, Orlando, FL

Design Concept: **Steve Schussler**

Consultant Designers: **Shea Architects, Minneapolis, MN**
JGA, Southfield, MI

Photography: **Bob Perzel, Perzel Photography Group**

Cleveland Indians Team Store

Galleria at Erieview Plaza, Cleveland, OH

Design: **Richard Jencen Assoc., Cleveland, OH**

Director of Design: **Nicholas Zalany**

Design Assistant: **Keith Royer**

Visual Merchandising: **Raymond Linhart**

For the Richard E. Jacobs Group

Project Coordinator: **William Rowe**

Visual Merchandising: **Jayne Churchmach**

When the Cleveland Indians took up residence in the Jacobs Field facility, the owners wanted a design for their retail store that would recreate the excitement of Jacobs Field. Standing up front—as part of the storefront design—is a life-size, custom sculpted and molded batter, in position at the plate. The pedestal contains an internally-lit "home plate" and it is set in front of the figure for up-lighting.

The floor plan of the store is conceptually a baseball diamond. In the critical and central area of the space is the custom designed sales desk. As the central focal point, it incorporates the ceiling soffits, four way TV monitors and a mannequin. From a functional standpoint, this unit eases the

traffic flow by directing traffic in two distinct directional flows. "It also allows the symmetry of uninterrupted merchandise display at the sidewalls."

Seen throughout the store are the custom designed fixtures which allow freedom of store design, planning and merchandising. Starting with the metalwork at the side walls, overhead trusses are tied in with fixturing to organize and departmentalize the merchandise. Integrated into the decorative steelwork are the baseball action graphics and the perimeter accent lighting. This brings the track lighting closer to the merchandise and also simplifies the reflected ceiling lighting layout.

"Merchandising played an important role in the overall store design." In keeping with the baseball theme, there is high level merchandising at the perimeter walls and coordinated related goods are displayed on the custom floor units. For "grandstand" appeal, the fast selling, fitted baseball caps are set out on a stepped sidewall display.

Ozone

North Point Mall, Atlanta, GA

Design: **Gary Aldridge & Associates, Roswell, GA**

The Ozone Electronics store was designed by Gary Aldridge & Assoc. of Roswell, GA for "the affluent and discriminating customer such as star athletes, corporate executives, and individual entrepreneurs" looking for small, one-of-a-kind or limited production "electronic toys." The stock in-store includes personal message centers, miniature video cameras, pocket-size note pads, etc.

Though the design is sleek and contemporary, the life-size cut-outs of stars of the Braves baseball team adds a sports-oriented attitude to the design. The serpentine walls and custom designed display towers with internal lighting for extra added attention and eye appeal all create a unique and distinctive setting for the unique and distinctive merchandise.

The lights in the towers are synchronized to fade from one color into another at a set speed so that there is a constant feeling of animation in the space. Adding to the "entertainment" are the TV monitors replaying sporting events and the swirling, glowing light across the ceiling that helps to set the look for the store through the mainly glazed facade. Light and air are the essence of Ozone.

Atlanta Braves Clubhouse Store

Northpoint Mall, Atlanta, GA

Design: **Gary Aldridge & Associates, Roswell, GA**

To promote and sell the Atlanta Braves logo merchandise, Gary Aldridge & Associates designed this open mall store based on the "simplicity of the team's locker room and the individual players."

From the mall, the shopper sees the overhead signage which features a neon lit logo plus blue metal streamers, also neon outlined, that stream out to either side of the sign and they are highlighted with actual baseballs. The team's colors—red and white—make up the color scheme of the store and the dark green plastic grass matting on the floor suggests the baseball field. A set of plexiglass, life-size cut-outs with black and white artwork are set atop the red showcase fixtures which features the Brave-inscribed products. From the entrance the viewer sees the batter at the plate—the pitcher in mid store and one of the outfielders near the rear of the store.

The perimeter walls are simply fixtured with an industrial pipe system finished in red. Above the light trough that illuminates the wall displays products are display arrangements of garments and memorabilia. There is one stall that is set aside to commemorate Hall of Famer, Hank Aaron.

Dropped ceiling panels of dark blue are also outlined in red neon while red metal shades on pendant light fixtures add to the locker-room look while also adding to the warm ambient light. Ceiling tracks light up the fascia displays.

NASCAR
Thunder Store

Gwinnett Mall, Atlanta, GA

Design: **Jon Greenberg Associates, Southfield, MI**

C.E.O.: **Michael Crosson**

Manager in Charge: **Michael O'Neil**

Senior Designer: **Jon Ebersole**

Project Manager: **Lori Nemeth**

Interior Design: **Jeri Bademian**

Job Captain: **Paul Frahm**

Graphics: **Tony Camilletti, V.P., Valentino Fischione, Graphic Designer**

Photography: **Gaylord Entertainment: In-House**

NASCAR Thunder brings the thunder—the roar—the thrills and excitement of racing zooming into the mall. As designed by Jon Greenberg Associates, the mall shopper feels the roar of the engines, sees the flash of the rippling checkered flag and the blast of the take off.

The storefront design is dominated by a floor-to-ceiling black and white checkered flag—the icon of car racing. Customers are steered into the store past the flag man on the high perch. The shopper passes by an authentic NASCAR race car in one front window while the other features a mural of cars racing towards the shopper and the entrance. Overhead is the store's sign and the Thunder logo with a dynamic lightening bolt.

Under an exposed darkened ceiling, "car haulers" are packed into the space. They are realistically executed with steel cladding, running lights, tire wells and fleet graphics from sponsoring corporations. The "haulers" are totally merchandised and flexible with components from other fixture systems used throughout the store.

On the opposite side of the space are the "pit stops" with gypboard canopies and heavy girders. Perforated metal wall systems, here, are interchangeable and give the space an authentic quality.

Feature floor fixtures, designed by JGA, suggest mechanic related objects such as tool boxes, tripod jacks, hydraulic cranes, etc. To continue the racetrack imagery part of the floor is "faux asphalt" and the balance is finished with recycled tires. High tech, industrial materials are used throughout to enhance the racetrack setting and the imagery is further strengthened by the bold palette of red, yellow, black and silvery chrome.

Adding to the "you are there" entertainment values of the store is the large multi-screen wall as the rear of the space. Great sports moments and chilling near misses are shown on the screens and the effect is heightened by the sound system that fills the store with the roars, gasps and cheers. Together they provide "the true drama and sensory layer necessary to complete the total experience."

The product line includes casual branded garments, tee shirts, posters, replica car hoods, emblems, racing paraphernalia and racing memorabilia. Tony Camilletti, V.P. of Communications for JGA who was involved in the graphic design for NASCAR Thunder said, "This is a store where it is difficult to tell where the design ends and the merchandising begins." Meanwhile, car racing enthusiasts can enjoy the experience of separating the two—if they want to.

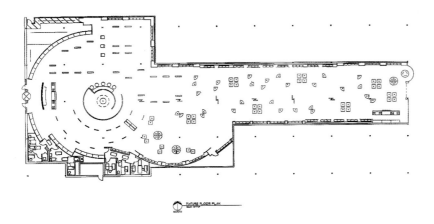

Daytona PitShop

**Daytona International Speedway,
Daytona, FL**

Design: **JGA, Southfield, MI**

CEO/Partner in Charge: **Michael Crosson**

Planner/Designer: **Michael Curtis**

Project Manager: **Edward Kaffel**

Photography: **Laszlo Regos, Berkley, MI**

The newly-opened exhibition hall in the new Daytona International Speedway captures and personifies the "essence of speed and race cars." Part of the hall is devoted to interactive attractions and historical exhibits while another part houses a retail shop filled with racing memorabilia, emblematic wearables, and novelty merchandise. The PitShop was created to "reflect celebrity drivers and racing."

An expanse of black and white checkered tile pattern flows into the store from the spacious common area and it represents one of the many racing references used in the design. The flooring transitions frequently throughout the space from bright primary racing colors to the use of more subtle charcoal carpeting. The exposed ceiling "features inspiration from the inner workings of a racing engine, using tubular lighting and ductwork to imply patterns of wiring and fluid lines." Custom metal "piston" display fixtures fitted with cut-out "head gasket" ceiling elements floating directly above serve as focal units in the store.

The circular shapes are also open to the space above which allows visitors to look down into the store from the second level. Along with "red toolbox"-inspired fixtures that serve as platforms, there are curvilinear

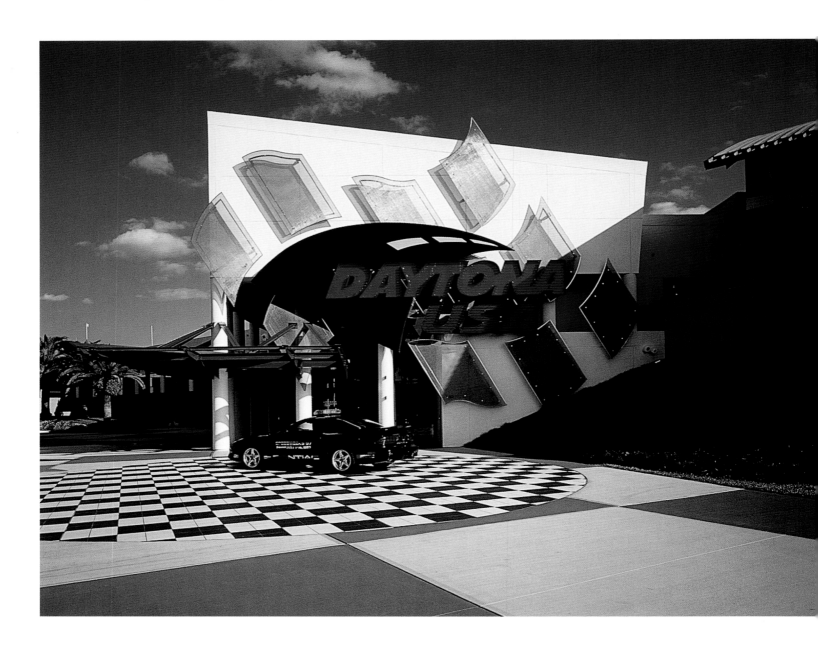

and modular metal floor fixtures and
perimeter wall systems. These are
galvanized and then finished with
a wheeled brush "for a stronger,
industrial 'mechanic shop' feeling."

As a draw to the primary focal
area and the cash/wrap area there
is a vivid and dynamic graphic which
depicts the pace and action of racing.
"The PitShop roars with the thrill
of the crowd and excites the car
aficionados with products and textures that create an extension of
the racing experience."

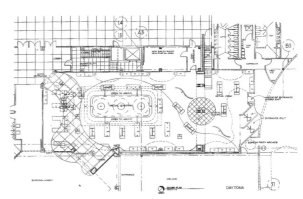

"Our goal was to bring a piece of the Indianapolis Motor Speedway to downtown Indianapolis"—so this store, designed by AAD (Associates in Architecture & Design) of Phoenix was opened.

Out in front is a "winged wheel" speedway logo and bricks, pulled from the original pre-World War II speedway, were built into the entrance floor. This sets the look for the store which "used authentic Speedway icons that reference race history." In the right and left flanks of the storefront the designers created sandblasted signs with graphics of famous Indy events such as the Backyard 500. Blade signs that resemble the chalked "gasoline left" or "laps to go" placards are used to point customers to the different areas inside the store.

One of the major focal points is the scoreboard pylon and another is the skid marks on the sealed concrete floor that leads to the actual Guerrero Indy car that sits in a checkered winning circle near the entrance. Contributing to the racing excitement are the multi-screen, digital video and stereo systems and the track-like catch fencing. Some of the displayers are designed to look like carts used in Gasoline Alley and to hang some featured apparel, a historical scoring pagoda is used.

Documenting the history of the Indy races and also establishing the authenticity of the logo and branded apparel and souvenirs are the racing helmets and graphics of the trophies won by the drivers. Upon exiting, photographic murals give the illusion of walking from Gasoline Alley back to the track.

Indianapolis Motor Speedway Store

Indianapolis, IN

Design: **AAD, Phoenix, AZ**

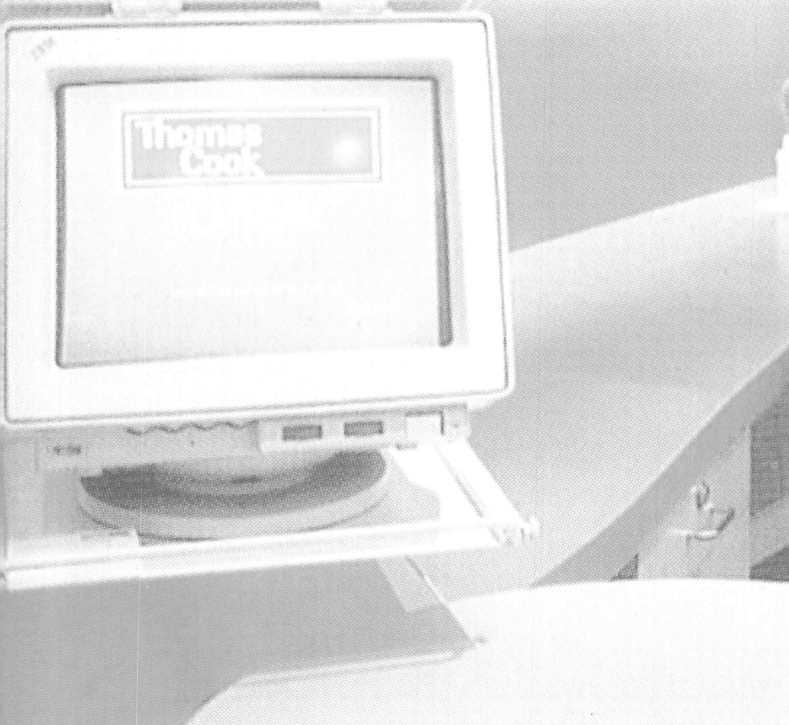

Potpourri

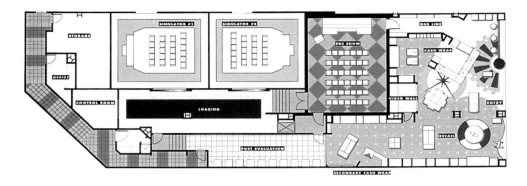

**TEMPUS ENTERTAINMENT
MALL OF AMERICA PLAN**

DECEMBER 10, 1994
Not to scale

The prototype for Tempus Expeditions, created by the Cincinnati office of FRCH Design Worldwide, offers a combination of entertainment, education and retailing in a dramatically-themed environment. The "entertainment and education" is combined in a high definition digital image presentation with #-D virtual audio, electronic motion simulation and exciting special effects that "immerses guests in a series of thrilling adventures that chronicle human ingenuity." These elements are reinforced in the selection of thematically-related merchandise sold in the 2300 sq. ft. retail area, up front.

The "drive to achieve" is represented by the larger than life figure leaping through the front glass—to get into Tempus. The giant gears suspended over the entry and repeated on the floor beneath symbolizes "human invention" and a statue of Venus stands under a domed moonhole cut into the ceiling where she is being observed by famous creators. "With its vibrant colors, rich detailing and imaginative themes, the

Tempus Expedition

Mall of America, Bloomington, MN

Design: **FRCH Design Worldwide, Cincinnati, OH**

retail component has been designed to intrigue mall shoppers passing by as well as Tempus customers before and after they have experienced the motion simulator ride.

While waiting to get into the "adventure" customers browse the store and its assortment of related merchandise all tied in with the theme or branded with the specially created Tempus logo. After the ride and after the post-evaluation area where riders can enter their reactions on video monitors and interact with high-tech, video gadgetry, they are "led" back to the retail space. the cash/wrap desk is accentuated by an imposing double arch that symbolizes man's architectural accomplishments and the large screen, high definition, video wall shows trailers of Tempus' latest attractions.

The concept is being fine tuned in the Mall of America with future retail/entertainment facilities in the planning.

Transporter

New York, NY

Design: **Brennan Beer Gorman Monk, New York, NY**

Principal in Charge: **Julia Monk, AIA, ASID**

Architect: **Richard Truemner**

Graphic Designer: **Katie Brennan-Smith**

Designer: **Ted Brumleve**

Lighting Design: **Susan Brady Lighting Design, Inc., New York, NY**

Photography: **Paul Warchol, New York, NY**

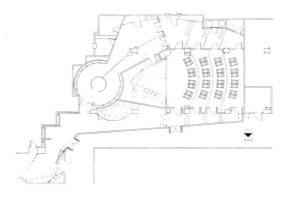

"Transporter: Movies you ride" has been envisioned as "a total immersion entertainment experience, transporting patrons through a series of interactive spaces on their journey to the main event: the motion simulation theater show." It functions as its own movie set, pre-show video briefing room and retail shop. It is located in the 4500 sq. ft. concourse level of the Empire State Bldg. And all the exposed plumbing, electrical wiring and ductwork are left exposed to "support the urban, post apocalyptic design."

The "adventure" starts at the Transporter sign imbued with fiber optic pulsating light and an immense video screen that greets patrons. Overlapping steel panels—lined up in forced perspective—lead to the next "set" where blue radon light can be seen behind perforated steel panels that curve around the prep room. A central ring of video monitors is interrupted by an artificially created "beam of daylight" that streams through it. "Wind simulators, fog machines, glistening red painted walls, artificial flames, wire mesh fencing and deep rumblings tickle the senses and heighten visitors' anticipation.

There is no way the "all shook up" Transporter rider can miss the Retail Shop as he exits from the 32-seat theater where each seat is hydraulically powered and moves 320 degrees per second mimicking and reinforcing the on-screen video action. The setting of the exit shop where souvenirs can be purchased continues the eerie and apocalyptic feeling of the space with high tech, industrial materials combined with dramatic lighting effects.

The simple inanimate shelves on the rear wall and the grid covered cabinets that make up the base of the curved service desk contain the folded merchandise.

Toys'R'Us

Raritan, NJ

Design: **Shea Architects, Minneapolis, MN**

Team Directors: **Christine Plantan & Greg Rothweiler**

Project Director: **Ed Wilms**

Project Manager: **Joel Springer**

Project Architect: **Kenneth Potts**

Design Team: **Maria Jordan/Ginny Latham/
Chris Harkman/Peter Rotundo/Janet Smith/
Rolly Stevens/Marcia Jorganson/Faith Hodkiewicz/
Paul Melblom**

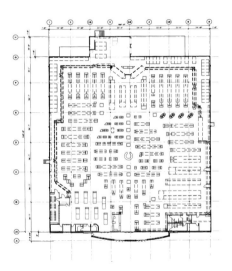

The task facing the Shea Architects of Minneapolis was to take an already world renown and successful operation, Toys'R'Us, and make it more user-friendly while also making it more in tune with the times. Customer research told the company that shoppers needed more reasons to shop at Toys'R'Us before heading to the larger malls.

This design, called Concept 2000, is a more friendly and a more cutting edge design that will become part of the company's national roll-out plans. One of the main attributes of the new design is that it increases the selling space by 10-20% by re-thinking how the store is stocked.

Now quick-moving items are allotted additional shelf space and staging areas store merchandise on rolling racks—ready to move as needed. The new, user-friendly white fixtures are set up around a yellow tile racetrack oval with the information desk centrally located. The oval aisle exposes shoppers to the various supergroups set out in the 44,500 sq. ft. big box store. According to Greg Rothweiler of Shea Architects, "Now it really does look like a big toy store with fun, animation, friendliness and accessibility that was missing in the previous, rigid aisle approach. Now it is fun to shop."

Geoffrey the Giraffe, the store's mascot, has been transformed and given more prominence. He and other larger-than-life 3-D icons have been added into the store's new design. "These three-dimensional icons help both children and adults recognize where they need to go as soon as they walk into the store"—just past the 12 ft. diameter Geoffrey logo set into the tile floor. The exposed ceiling is painted white and filled with halogen pendant fixtures. The tile floor contains a variety of bright and happy colors many keyed in with the departmental signage which also is bright and colorful in the open space.

Setting the tone for the new concept store is the ceiling-to-floor curving storefront in bright blue gridded with clear yellow. Geoffrey makes a stellar appearance atop the facade along with the familiar multi-colored Toys'R'Us logo. "Geoffrey is a fun element that gives a sense of playfulness to the store and helps strengthen our identity as Toys'R'Us," said Mike Gerety, VP of Store Planning for Toys'R'Us. "We needed to make a change—and maybe something dramatic—and to differentiate ourselves in a much stronger way. We wanted to create a 'WOW' factor."

Zoom Toy Store

**Crown Center Shops,
Kansas City, MO**

Design: **Glynn Brown Design, Kansas City, MO**

President: **Glynn Brown, ASID**

VP: **Jim Clay**

Photography: **Architectura Photo Graphics, Paul S. Kivet**

Zoom is a toy store targeted at children and adults alike, and the Glynn Brown Design firm has created a fun and fantasy land to delight all.

The designers have literally interpreted the client's wishes and the store has a "fun, unusual look—and it is a great background for the merchandise." Somewhere in the 2100 sq. ft. space there is a clearly thought out and executed store design that is secondary to the merchandise presentation. The owner, John Middlecamp, likes to keep his stores "small in size, but big in ingenuity," and his merchandise is geared towards the upscaled customer.

The logo literally and figuratively ZOOMS across the entrance way—outlined in neon—and supported by decorative curved piers. Inside, the exposed ceiling has been painted black and is covered with dropped red lacquered grids and striped with the ceiling tracks that light up the

space. Combined with the additional drop lights over the cash/wrap, the tracklights provide "a great latitude in highlighting the merchandise." The grids make it easy to suspend and dangle merchandise from the ceiling: adding color and excitement to the store's ambience.

The turquoise colored cement floor is dripped and splattered with color a la Jackson Pollack to affect a bright, colorful and easy to maintain floor. A raised portion of the selling floor is tile carpeted and it is accessible by a ramp. The simple white metal frame and grid floor fixtures are defined by painted and angled end pieces in pink, coral and red that add bright vertical emphasis in warm colors to the interior. Some perimeter walls are finished with slatwall for ease of merchandising and flexibility in accommodating new products.

The Game Keeper

Escondito, CA

Design: **Perkins Freund Partnership, Santa Monica, CA**

Design: **Janet Perkins**

Architect: **Don Freund**

Photography: **Perkins Freund Partnership & M.P./RVC**

The fun and fancy that typifies the merchandise to be found in the Game Keeper store is presented out front in the large scale graphics that make up the facade of the mall-situated store. The graphics "express the playful, dynamic imagery" and "the exaggerated scale of the sign and architectural elements serve as a frame for the small scale merchandise."

The designers took advantage of the 17 ft. height of the store front and expanded the sign to "a monumental scale." The Queen is positioned in the center for maximum impact and the shopper must move around her to enter which suggests the "interacting with the game." The dart over the corrugated "Keeper" sign emphasizes the height of the front. It is also used "to poke fun at the perfect symmetry of the facade."

The center axis of symmetry is continued inside the 1200 sq. ft., beautifully-illuminated space and the overall ambience says that there are "games" to be played. Here, the interpretation of the game imagery is more literal and includes black and white checkerboards on the cash/wrap desk and on the illuminated, raised ceiling, and the red metal disks atop the columns that clearly separate the different classifications of games resemble giant poker chips. They carry some of the signage that clearly tells the shopper where which games can be found. Giant dice appear on the dark gray industrial carpeted floor and they serve as display tables.

The fixturing is made of clear maple, white laminates and red highlights. Like the red poker chips that project like blade signs from the wall, the classification signs over the wall shelves are also red with white lettering. "The colors of all the materials are in the warm ranges to create an inviting playground in which to have fun."

Travelfest Superstore

Austin, TX

Design: **Alamo Architects, San Antonio, TX**

Architectural Design: **Billy Lawrence/Mike McGlone/Fernando Ortega**

Artist: **Alex Brochon**

Photography: **Paul Bardagjy Photography**

The Alamo Architects created the look and physical being for Travelfest—a new chain of travel and travel/retail accessories. With its "airport"-like ambience and the "departure gates" to different parts of the world where the shopper can actually find travel books, videos and maps for sale, the experience starts the adventure here in the planning stage. The ticketing is done in-store, at an airport counter and on the sales floor there are airport dollies loaded with travel related merchandise for sale.

This is the second store and it is a further development of the original prototype design. The 10,000 sq. ft. former auto showroom has been converted into an exciting, thematic space that combines actual travel service and merchandise with travel imagery. Travel agents sit in custom designed work stations below a mural of the world as viewed from the North Pole. The airline tickets are picked up at the airport counter. An airplane "wing" of perforated aluminum supports the lighting, the neon and the signage and it extends through the store. It also creates an entrance canopy. Books and merchandise are contained in small, special-ized areas which are identified by a 2x2 drop, painted murals and airbrushed light fixture globes as well as Dura-trans sign cabinets.

Billy Lawrence, a partner in Alamo Architects said, "We concentrated on creating a concourse and circulating customers through it after getting them from the street into the store. " "We arranged it so there is always an interest to keep them moving—but no prescribed way to do it," added Mike McGlone, another partner.

In this store there are additional travel agent stations, and the Learning Center and Geo-Fun Kids areas have also been expanded. The architects added new attractions such as fiber optic signs that identify cities and destinations and TV monitors that show travel videos. Gary Hoover, the entrepreneur who is the brainchild behind Travelfest said, "A store must offer something that a customer can't get at home—making the physical space more important now than ever. The internet can never be a showcase."

Thomas Cook

Boston, Lincolnshire, England

Design: **Red Jacket, London, England**

The new retail concept for the venerable Thomas Cook travel agency is currently being tested in the Boston, Lincolnshire store designed by Red Jacket, a London-based design firm. According to Keith Hendry, Visual Merchandising Manager for Thomas Cook, the reaction from both old and new customers has been extremely positive. The new, informal, relaxing colors and the open and more inv iting space design have made the please of planning a trip even more pleasurable.

The signature red of Thomas Cook is very evident on the store's facade enlivening the High Street location. Inside the red is complemented by purple, yellow and blue; an all new and untraditional color palette for an established, tradition filled company.

The often stand-offish counter is no longer a barrier between agent and customer who now share a table, chairs and a swiveling computer screen. The design team worked closely with Keith Hendry of Cook's to make the visit as enjoyable and comfortable for the client and the family as it is profitable for the agency. Children aren't forced to sit quietly and mind their manners but are welcome to crawl about on the colorful floor or sit before a TV monitor and enjoy specially selected films. The more "sophisticated" youngsters can play with provided Nintendo Game Boys.

The poster clutter is gone from the front windows and shoppers on the street get a welcome view into the bright, colorful store. Passing through the double doors, the client is greeted by a "maitre d'" who assists and directs the prospective customer. In a comfortable seating area, they can study brochures while awaiting personal service.

The brochures are displayed on racks that resemble book shelves. Travel videos have been adapted, put on computer tape, and shown on a screen set on the shelf amidst the brochures. Destination videos provide a source of education as well as entertainment shown on larger monitors near the Foreigh Currency desk.

Even the music that fills the air was carefully selected and is frequently changed especially since it does affect the agent who works all day in the store. As the day ends the music gets to be more "up." To come are destination video stations with which the client can interact using buttons on the screen.

The new, brighter color palette, open plan, individualized attention, concern for client's comfort and convenience and the entertainment factor have made a trip to Thomas Cook as much fun as the trip planned by Thomas Cook.

FAO Schweetz

Watertower, Michigan Ave., Chicago, IL

Design: **J. Newbold & Assoc., Inc., New York, NY**

Designer: **Joanne Newbold**

Graphic Design: **John Kehe**

Producer of Construction Documents: **AAD, Phoenix, AZ**

Architect: **Timothy Pleger**

The new FAO Schwarz concept store—FAO Schweetz—is a "dream come true for kids of all ages—a candy heaven on earth." This store design which either shares space with the noted toy store or stands alone as it does in the Watertower in Chicago, is a treat for all the senses. It is bright color, fun, imagination, animation, lights and wonderful sweet delights in bulk containers or pre-packaged for easy shopping.

The floor is laid out like a giant Candyland playing board with colorful blocks of tiles snaking in and around the floor fixtures that are also colorful and bright. Up near the front is a nine ft. tall chocolate soldier and a gummy bear totem pole. The adventure filled stroll through this "giant gumball machine" takes the shopper through the lollipop forest and past a chorus line of Jelly Belly Beans strutting their stuff as they highlight the myriad flavors of jelly beans in the glistening glass cylinders beneath them. The three dimensional, animated "gummy aquarium" is designed to look like a giant diving helmet. Here, "gummy fish, sharks, worms, and other creep crawly creatures provide delicious bait for the unsuspecting candy diver."

M&Ms Colorworks (trademarked) prominently appears in FAO Schweetz

with a rainbow of 24 individual colors highlighted by new "stars" in gold, silver, pink, aqua and lavender. Two animated M&M characters carry on a fun-filled conversation to the delight of the children held in rapt attention.

For the serious choco-holic there is FAO Schweetz Chocolate Mint where "gold bricks" of Godiva Chocolates are contained in a "vault" guarded by a chocolate soldier. The vault carries the "Godiva at FAO Schweetz" signage and it signifies a first for Godiva and will probably lead to a line of co-branded products.

Forty four different flavors of "sours" are found in the Sour Patch Fruit Stand. Bushel baskets and seed-packet signage—along with talking sour faced characters "redefine the concept of a sour-face." The adventure ends—as all games must—at the Weigh-In Station: the checkout counter. The scale makes a loud announcement full of hoots, toots, whistles and shouts—based on how much candy is being weighed. It makes a fitting and fun finale for the entertaining experience and best of all—there is still the candy to be eaten at leisure.

This design has won numerous design awards for its colorful, imaginative and unique solution for a store design under 5000 sq. ft.

Fuzziwig's

Arizona Factory Mall, Phoenix, AZ

Design: **Jay B. Haws, VP of Marketing**

Developed by: **Rocky Mountain Chocolate Factory, Inc.**

President: **Franklin E. Crail**

Photography: **Ron Schwager, Chico, CA**

Fuzziwig's is a 1200 sq. ft. retail store offering self-service bulk candies, soft drinks, logo merchandise—and entertainment. "We believe that interactive and entertainment shopping is the future of retailing in this country," said Jay Haws, VP of Marketing for the Rocky Mountain Chocolate Factory. "Usual props, animated characters, lighting, sound and color create a memorable theme to attract and keep customers of all ages."

Blending reality, fantasy and nostalgia, Haws created Prof. Fuzziwig who embodies the genius of Willy Wonka; the inventive wackiness of Doc Emmet Brown; and the mischievous spirit of Santa Claus. In the "candy factory" interior," the animated figures, and moving machinery, create a kinetic ambience that amuses—and sells the products.

The factory concept is foremost in the design's execution. All shapes are rounded or radiused, and all surfaces are bordered by simulated strapping with heavy duty "rivets." Tarnished copper, faux verdigris, antique maroon and gold serve as foils for the bright, strong colors of the candies. Light, sound and motion surround the shopper in the store.

There is festive music played against the clickety-clack of the "machinery" and the lively lighting creates drama and depth and directs shoppers to the highlighted merchandise.

The shopper can watch the Fuzzimobile as it sends fresh fruits through an overhead conveyor to descend down a chute into the Fuzzijuicer: a converted claw-footed bathtub where the fruit is "stomped" into juice. The juice is drained off, "boiled in bubbling water beakers and then distilled into exotic flavors." After sugar has been added, the juice "through a secret process is magically transformed into every sweet delight imaginable." The candy is then transported overhead and distributed along tubes down to the glass bulk candy bins that line the perimeter walls.

In the window—facing the mall—boys and girls can meet Kayo, an impish monkey who operates the Fuzzimixer that makes an assortment of candies. He invites the children and their parents to enter. Inside, in addition to the candy, there are souvenir Fuzziwig T-shirts and propeller caps as well as mylar and latex occasion balloons. A line of ancillary Fuzziwig merchandise is being developed.

Great Cars, Great Trucks

Mall of America, Bloomington, MN

Design: **Fitch, Worthington, OH**

Project Managers:

Mark Artus: Fitch Christine MacKenzie: Chrysler Corp.

Bib Abele/John Howard/Jeff Bickerstaff: Ross Roy Communications

Designers: **Mark Artus/Christian Davies/ Jon Baines/Fred Goode/Jacquie Richmond/ Paul Lycett/Randy Miller**

Photography: **Mark Steele**

Only a few years old and already the Mall of Americas has become a leading retail/entertainment destination that rivals both Disney World and the Grand Canyon combined. Since more than half of the retail stores in this mall are prototypes, the Chrysler Corp. decided it was the place to test its new idea—and get the public's reaction.

Great Cars, Great Trucks is named after the new corporate image campaign. The Fitch Company working with Ross Roy Communications—one of Chrysler's agencies—developed a permanent display/auxiliary retail space that translated the campaign's key message into an entertainment filled, 3-D experience. "It's important for people to be able to touch and feel the cars and remain anonymous and not threatened," said Christine MacKenzie of the Chrysler Corp. Since cars and trucks are not actually sold here, visitors can feel comfortable looking, touching and trying. The 15,000 sq. ft. area in the Mall of America showcases Chrysler's latest concept and production cars, trucks, minivans and utility vehicles.

At the entrance is a concept or image car: the Chrysler 300 concept car was featured at the recent opening. A winding hardwood "bridge" gently steers the visitors away from the activities of the mall into a refined setting with art deco design, soft music, multi-media technology and lifestyle product displays. Within the space there is an abundance of interactive technology including terminals linked to the Worldwide Web, a video theater, video games for kids and hands-on displays such as the Jeep Wrangler driving simulator.

Visitors can use the computers to help determine which is the best Chrysler product for their needs. Within a 2000 sq. ft. retail space visitors can enjoy shopping for clothing, models, games, toys, and other Chrysler-related merchandise.

The lifestyle displays include a rugged outdoor vignette for the heavy duty vehicles, one for sports car enthusiasts, a more elegant setting for luxury cars as well as one for the "average family."

Though vehicle displays will be changed frequently—to encourage more repeat visits—the Dodge Viper RT/10 or GTS Coupe will stay on as "an icon of Chrysler's new image and its vision of automotive manufacturing today."

The Fitch team was responsible for the interior space design, environmental graphics, custom fixturing and display set-ups as well as developing several of the interactive media programs.